All Creation Sings

All Creation Sings

The Voice of God in Nature

J. Ellsworth Kalas

Abingdon Press
Nashville

Library of Congress Cataloging-in-Publication Data

Kalas, J. Ellsworth, 1923-
   All creation sings : the voice of God in nature / J. Ellsworth Kalas.
      p.   cm.
   ISBN 978-1-4267-0791-9 (binding: pbk./trade, adhesive perfect : alk. paper)   1. Nature in the Bible.   I. Title.
   BS660.K35 2010
   220.8′508—dc22

2010000534

10 11 12 13 14 15 16 17 18 19—10 9 8 7 6 5 4 3 2 1

MANUFACTURED IN THE UNITED STATES OF AMERICA

To Bill and Carol Latimer,

in honor of the generosity with which

you have blessed many worthy causes,

and in profound gratitude for

your ministry to the students of

Asbury Theological Seminary

CONTENTS

CONTENTS

FOREWORD

In a recent Christmas season, while a group of us were caroling in several retirement communities and nursing homes, I found myself in a conversation with two of the carolers, my friends Jon and Lyn Akers. Lyn said, "I wish you'd write a book on 'This Is My Father's World.'" I knew the hymn to which she was referring and the theme she had in mind. "You're right," I answered. "In truth, I've given some thought to the idea and even have a small file of materials." I took Lyn's word as the prompting of the Spirit and went to work. This book is the result.

Early in my writing I was surprised by a letter and package from Jayne Thompson Hart, who had been part of my congregation at the First United Methodist Church in Madison, Wisconsin, roughly forty years ago when she was a graduate student at the University of Wisconsin. She wanted me to see a book that had contributed to her thinking as both a scientist and a believer, *The Sacred Depths of Nature* by Professor Ursula Goodenough. While the book—beautiful in its own right—differs with some of my own theological convictions, it stimulated and blessed my thinking. The timing of Jayne's letter and gift would seem to some to be a pleasant coincidence; for me it was Providence. I am grateful.

We humans live in the midst of wonders, and it seems clear that we are the only creatures with the capacity to examine, analyze, and then use and abuse this conglomerate of nature's miracles. I pray that this little book will help us look beyond nature's wonders to the God of creation—and then, with gratitude, to treat nature with the reverent sense of stewardship that God intended us humans to employ.

J. Ellsworth Kalas

CHAPTER 1

ALL NATURE SINGS

Scripture Reading: Job 38:1-11

Let me introduce you to Maltbie Babcock. It's rather likely that you've met him, even if his name isn't familiar or if you have no recollection of the meeting. He was a Christian minister—a Presbyterian, to be precise—and he packed a beautiful life and career into a short forty-three years. When he was the pastor at the Brown Memorial Presbyterian Church in Baltimore, he was so popular with the students at Johns Hopkins University that the university reserved a room where students could confer with him. He then succeeded Henry van Dyke, one of the most notable ministers of the time, as pastor of the Brick Presbyterian Church in New York City. Still rather early in that pastorate, Babcock embarked on a trip to the Holy Land but died en route, in Naples, Italy.

I dare to say that you probably know him—as I do—for words that he may well have written relatively early in his ministerial career, though they weren't published until the year of his death. These words reflected the way he seemed always to feel about life and nature, but they found their encapsulating phrase during the years of his first pastorate in Lockport, New York. A person who found not only beauty but restorative strength in nature, Babcock cherished a spot at the top of a hill outside Lockport where he had an unspoiled view of Lake Ontario. As he would leave for a walk to that spot, Babcock's parting words would be, "I am going out to see my Father's world." Somewhere in the course of the years, Babcock put his feelings about his "Father's world" into a poem of sixteen stanzas. The poem was published in *Thoughts for Daily Living* in 1901. Some years later four of those stanzas became a hymn, with these words:

> This is my Father's world,
> and to my listening ears
> all nature sings, and round me rings
> the music of the spheres.
> This is my Father's world:
> he shines in all that's fair;
> in the rustling grass I hear him pass;
> he speaks to me everywhere.[1]

It is on the basis of this hymn—a hymn that has remained beloved for over a century—that I suggested you probably knew Maltbie Babcock even though you've never met him. One can't use another's phrases (and, indeed, be blessed by them) without forming an unconscious friendship with the author.

It is true still today that "all nature sings," but it is increasingly difficult to catch the melody. I haven't visited the spot in Lockport, New York, where Babcock got his hours of refreshment, but that quiet spot probably now has become either a suburban development or a shopping mall. And almost anywhere we go, for that matter, nature's voice is now muted by the sound of traffic and assorted electronic devices. Those who go out to walk or jog are likely to wear a device that keeps them in touch with news or music or speech, so that—intentionally or not—they have shut out nature's sound and dulled its influence. And of course I fear that many in our time who stop to hear nature sing will not come to Dr. Babcock's conclusion that they hear God pass in "the rustling grass," or that they sense God speaking to them everywhere.

Which brings me to the point of this book. I rejoice greatly in the "green" movement that has made new millions conscious of the wonder of our creation and the blessed necessity of caring for it passionately. This is a magnificent step in the right direction, and it puts quality content into what might otherwise be little more than sentimental feelings. But I want us to go further than that. I want us not simply to see—and indeed, to be grateful for—the wonders of nature, and to be responsible for their care. I want us to go beyond nature's exquisite beauty until we learn some of the lessons it would teach us, lessons about both life and God. When nature sings (as it does every moment), its melody draws us to God, if only we listen with our whole being.

This is the way the biblical writers saw the world around them, and the way they wanted all humankind to see it. And in truth most people in Dr. Babcock's day still were inclined to see the world that way, at least in a measure. A famous preacher of the late nineteenth century advised young preachers that, if they saw attention wandering during a sermon, they should take their congregations "out to the country," where the preachers could regain their congregations' interest by causing them to think about nature. I doubt that many public speakers would use such a device today to recapture the attention of a wandering audience. We postmoderns are more likely to find our lessons, figures of speech, and compelling interests in the world of sports, entertainment, business, industry, or politics.

Not so with the biblical writers. They found their greatest lessons in the world of nature. When the Old Testament writer wanted to explain the breathtaking extent of King Solomon's legendary wisdom, he put it this way: "He composed three thousand proverbs; and his songs numbered a thousand and five. He would speak of *trees,* from the cedar that is in the Lebanon to the *hyssop* that grows in the wall; he would speak of *animals,* and *birds,* and *reptiles,* and *fish*" (1 Kings 4:32-33; emphasis added). This was the biblical writer's ways of demonstrating Solomon's wisdom—not by a recitation of his academic degrees or of his economic or political astuteness, but as someone who understood nature and who found lessons and wisdom in her precincts. But Solomon wasn't unique in his holy fascination with nature. We think immediately of Jesus and of how often he made his teaching points with nature as his example. A certain man, he said, "went out to sow" (Matthew 13:3). He tells us of a shepherd who had "a hundred sheep and losing one of them" left the ninety-nine in the wilderness to pursue the lost one (Luke 15:3-4). And again, "Consider the lilies of the field, how they grow" (Matthew 6:28). It isn't surprising that Jesus used such language, because he was not only surrounded by nature, he had grown up hearing and praying the Psalms. His soul must have been saturated with phrases like, "The heavens are telling the glory of God; / and the firmament proclaims his handiwork" (Psalm 19:1), and "I lift up my eyes to the hills" (Psalm 121:1). I wonder how often Jesus might have looked at the hills around Nazareth and said, "You crown the year with your bounty; / your wagon tracks overflow with richness. / The pastures of the wilderness overflow, / the hills gird themselves with joy, / the meadows clothe themselves with flocks, / the valleys deck themselves with grain, / they shout and sing together for joy" (Psalm 65:11-13).

Through the centuries, devout and casual believers have seen God's hand in nature. We're told that as Baron von Hugel walked at night on the Wiltshire Downs, he would look up into the vast sky and cry out in awe, "God, God, God!" Geoffrey Chaucer described nature as "the vicaire of the almyghty lorde." Blaise Pascal exercised his usual capacity for summing up great insights in a few words: "Nature has some perfections to show that she is the image of God, and some defects to show that she is only His image." But it was Alfred Lord Tennyson who left us with one of the loveliest pictures in some of the most quoted lines:

Flower in the crannied wall,
I pluck you out of the crannies,
I hold you, root and all, in my hand,
Little flower—but *if* I could understand
What you are, root and all, and all in all,
I should know what God and man is.

Edna St. Vincent Millay saw God so near at hand in the wonders of nature—indeed, in even its most ordinary wonders—that she would write, "God, I can push the grass apart / And lay my finger on Thy heart."

But if nature is so much a gift of God that we can all but touch God in its beauty, and if Tennyson is right in feeling that a single, tiny, obscure flower can open our understanding of both God and humanity, it must nevertheless be said that we humans don't always read nature that well. The Apostle Paul said that the revelation of God in nature is so clear and powerful that we humans are "without excuse" if we fail to know God. Ever since the creation of the world, Paul said, God's eternal power and deity have been clearly shown in the things God has made. Nevertheless, Paul continued, we humans haven't necessarily found God in creation. We have looked at God's wonders, and instead of worshiping God, we have worshiped that which God has made. So it is that much primitive religion—and perhaps more postmodern thinking than we realize—have allowed nature to conceal God. Indeed, perhaps we have chosen to use it in such ways that we see nature as an end in herself, rather than as a voice that "sings" until around us "rings / The music of the spheres." It is altogether likely that we postmoderns are missing the best of God's creation. The music is everywhere, but we have allowed our souls to become tone-deaf.

Part of the problem lies in one of the very creatures of nature, namely ourselves. We must remind ourselves that there is more to nature than wind and trees and sky. Human beings—people like you and me—are also part of nature. The psalmist said, "I am fearfully and wonderfully made" (Psalm 139:14). Unfortunately, it is only occasionally that we ponder the wonder that is wrapped up by our own skin, this composite of miracles that constitute you and me. Sometimes we stumble on the fact unwillingly when illness takes us to the physician's office, where we discover how intricately all our parts come together and how important is some little, previously unknown part. And then again, at those times when weariness takes us from high optimism to the edge of despair, we realize that even the simplest of us is more delicately put together than the most sophisticated computer.

The especially fascinating and challenging factor in us humans is this, that we are decision-makers; we are creatures who make choices—and therefore creatures with the ability to determine not only our own fate but also to influence the fate and degree of happiness of many others. Indeed, it is in our power to shape the course of our planet; now, in fact, to reach beyond our own planet and to corrupt or bless the wider spheres. This quality makes us different from the rest of nature. The tree, the wind, the sky seem to do as they are told. They're programmed in quite astonishing ways, and they follow this programming faithfully so that they perform as trees and winds and skies should. As some preacher said a long generation ago, it's proper to chide a young man by saying, "Act like a man!" but no one needs to tell a tiger, "Act like a tiger!"

It's this power of choice that distinguishes us from the creation around us. I'm told that a great Bible teacher at the turn of the twentieth century once described the creation as a majestic symphony. As each part of nature was finished—light, darkness, land, water, plants, animals—the symphony was melodic beyond imagination, with harmony as enchanting as eternity. And with each progression in the creation story, the harmony mounted until at last it reached a peak in the shaping of the human creature, the crowning element in the process. But then, suddenly and with no warning, there was a discord in the universe, a frightening, off-key chaos of sound. It was the sound of our human re-bellion. We broke the harmony of nature. We disrupted the symphony.

The Apostle Paul insisted that "what can be known about God is plain," because God has shown it through cre-ation. "Ever since the creation of the world [God's] eternal power and divine nature, invisible though they are, have been understood and seen through the things he has made." Nevertheless, we humans—"without excuse"—"did not honor him as God or give thanks to him"; instead, we "be-came futile" in our thinking, until our "senseless minds were darkened. Claiming to be wise," we "became fools" (Romans 1:19-22).

These are hard words. Some might hasten to argue that Paul is talking specifically about the way primitive cultures have chosen to make graven images of particular animals or birds, or to bow before the sun, the moon, or the stars. But I think it is right and fair to extend Paul's words to the way our generation, in all too many acts and attitudes, has responded to its own growing knowledge of nature. Oscar Wilde defined a cynic as someone "who knows the price of everything and the value of nothing." We are in danger of doing something like that with nature—of losing the ulti-mate values and wonders of creation in the statistics, the chemical structures, and the predictability of variations. Per-haps we are like the military advisor who felt that, when he had calculated the size of the enemy army and the distance they would have to march, felt he had already won the battle. Even so, we're likely to think that because we know so much about the content of nature, we have taken it by conquest.

There is so much more to nature, however, than any-thing we can grasp even with the most effective microscope or telescope. Perhaps Tennyson was overly romantic when he trembled before the "flower in the crannied wall," a thing so fragile that he could pluck it "out of the crannies" and yet so mysterious that he felt that if he could understand it, "root and all, and all in all," he would have invaded the grandest mysteries of God and of his own human nature. I repeat, perhaps he was overly romantic. So, too, with Joyce Kilmer when he declared that—poet though he was—he would never see "a poem lovely as a tree." But if Tennyson and Kilmer were overly romantic, I choose to be with them rather than with someone who feels that nature is simply something to be experienced in a ten-day trip, or someone who feels that in reciting the data of the stars, he or she has gone to the heart of the universe. To stop with such an understanding is, indeed, to be like spectacles without eyes.

Job, the protagonist of the Old Testament book that bears his name, went through a devastating series of losses and trials. As the tragedies mounted and as his well-meaning but quite insensitive friends only made matters worse, Job kept hoping for one thing—that he could make his case before his Creator. He needed to understand and to be understood, and he felt that if only he could get a proper audience with God, all else would be manageable.

God answered Job by first asking him a question: "Where were you when I laid the foundation of the earth?" (Job 38:4), after which God took him on a whirlwind tour of creation. At times the tour was marked by magnificence and at times by touches that were quite playful. At one point, God asks Job if he has ever "caused the dawn to know its place" (38:12), and at another time explains to Job the peculiar ways of the ostrich (39:13-18). When the trip is completed, Job confesses that he has seen "things too wonderful for me, which I did not know" (42:3). And with it all, Job declares, "I had heard of you by the hearing of the ear, / but now my eye sees you," and with this revelation, the great soul repented as he entered a new relationship with God (42:5-6).

Katherine Mansfield, one of the brightest young writers of the first quarter of the twentieth century, insisted again and again that she couldn't believe in a personal God. This sometimes left her with a painful void. On one particularly glorious day, she wrote to her husband, the critic and writer John Middleton Murry, "If only one could make some small grasshoppery sound of praise to *someone*—thanks to *someone*. But who?" When all nature sings, an honest heart like Ms. Mansfield's must indeed feel left out of the music, and bereft because of it. When all of creation seems to declare the glory of God, the human creature—the member of creation with the highest sensitivity for the eternal—ought surely to lead the music, even if with only a "small grasshoppery sound." I invite you to join your heart and voice to such a choir.

NOTE

1. Maltbie Babcock, "This Is My Father's World," *The United Methodist Hymnal* (Nashville: The United Methodist Publishing House, 1989), 144.

CHAPTER 2

THE STORY OF THE THREE TREES

Scripture Reading: Genesis 2:8-17

I will always be grateful to my fifth- or sixth-grade teacher (I'm sorry I don't know which), who required us to memorize Joyce Kilmer's poem "Trees." Its rhythm and rhyme are so simple that we're likely to miss the essential beauty of Kilmer's words and the reverence with which he wrote. Elementary science can tell us that some trees are taller than thirty-story buildings, and all of us know that many trees outlive human beings. I remember a sixty-year-old businessman who was planting a tiny sapling in his front yard. "You know why I'm doing this?" he asked, then answered his own question. "I'm planting it for Caroline [his ten-year-old adopted daughter]. Someday she will sit in its shade." If the tree were a giant sequoia, someone could sit beneath it two thousand years from now.

But Joyce Kilmer was thinking about more than such measurable data; he was recognizing the tree as a gift from God. I think Kilmer felt that God loved trees or else there wouldn't be such an investment of heaven in their beauty.

Trees have a holy history of their own. It is recorded for us in the Scriptures, beginning early in Genesis. There, we're told that our first ancestors had their address in a garden. The historian or the anthropologist may question this idea, but the average person will listen to Genesis with sensitive agreement. Something in us feels instinctively and innately at home in a garden. This is true even for those of us who have no particular urge to run our fingers through the soil or to root out weeds. I wonder if this feeling is older than history, older even than conscious memory. I wonder if it is a primeval feeling, more in our blood than in our brains. I wonder if, when we walk barefoot in the grass, we come closer to knowing the truth about ourselves and our origins than when we put on our spectacles in the library or bend tirelessly over the Internet.

The Bible doesn't tell us much about this garden. Ten thousand artists, poets, and assorted dreamers have enlarged upon the Bible's description for centuries, so that, when we read the Bible story, most of us rather automatically see it through the eyes of some of these interpreters. But all of this imagining seems to have its own endorsement in the Genesis story, when the writer says, "Out of the ground the LORD God made to grow every tree that is pleasant to the sight and good for food" (Genesis 2:9). That is, the garden provided not only food for our physical survival but also the beauty so necessary for the nourishment of our souls.

The late Walter Russell Bowie told about a Christmas a generation or two ago when, in the midst of financial depression, an organization was trying to serve the poor in a large city by meeting their basic survival needs. The organization received a letter from a woman who asked that something be done for a family who had once been prosperous but was now destitute. The letter explained that there was a little girl in the family who had previously enjoyed having a garden of her own but who was now living in a tenement. The letter mentioned several necessities which ought to be sent to the little girl, then concluded, "Oh, above all, send her one red rose."[1] The Bible lets us know that our first address was like that: a garden whose trees contained not only food necessary for existence but also "every tree that is pleasant to the sight." Ponder this the next time you see a flowering pear tree in bloom, or when it's cherry blossom time—or when a gingko tree takes sunshine into its leaves in the fall.

But it is neither the beauty nor the sustenance of trees that gives them their ultimate prominence in the Bible story. God's first word to the human creature is a word of warning—to be exact, a word of forbidding. "You may freely eat of every tree of the garden; but of the tree of the knowledge of good and evil you shall not eat, for in the day that you eat of it you shall die" (Genesis 2:16-17). Talk about poison ivy!

It's significant that Genesis describes this tree as being "in the middle of the garden" (Genesis 3:3 NEB). That's appropriate because this tree is the crisis point, the very issue of the garden. It is the place at which we human creatures exercised our unique humanness. The great American poet Robert Frost spoke of "two roads diverged in a yellow wood," and how he took one, "And that has made all the difference."[2] Adam and Eve could have said as much; they had a choice and they took it, and the choice was at that tree "in the middle of the garden." Symbolically, this tree was (and is) at the very center of life, a place where it can't be missed, where the excitement of its offering is right in our path, where it insists on being considered.

But this was the one tree whose fruit was forbidden. The prohibition was so crucial that Adam had been warned that the day anyone ate of the tree, that person would surely die. I won't try to analyze the full meaning of this tree or of the restriction so vigorously laid around it—partly, I confess, because I don't understand its full meaning! But at the least, recognize that the tree was the point at which Adam and Eve exercised free will. This was the place where they made a choice—the classic choice, of whether to believe God or to believe life's other enticing voices; and with it, the choice whether to obey or to disobey God. It was, that is, the test of obedience. And at this tree, Adam and Eve flaunted God's wishes.

Whatever that tree means historically, for you and me it represents the continuing issue of *decision*. That is, this tree is not simply a long-ago event in the story of someone named Adam and Eve, nor is it simply an ancient fable. It is your story and mine. It is the locale of every struggle between good and evil. It is last week's business decision, last night's dinner party, this morning's flare of selfishness with a friend or family member. As such, this tree grows in living room, family room, bedroom, and kitchen. It grows in the shopping mall, in the coffee shop, in the stadium and the playing field of every sporting event. It is present in the periodical we read, the music to which we listen, the Internet where we spend life's irreplaceable resource, time. This tree grows wherever any son or daughter of earth decides that he or she will have his or her own way, and God go hang. This tree is symbolic of all our human trouble because it is symbolic of the ultimate issue of what a human being is: you and I are decision-makers. We make choices. We determine fates. We influence the fate of other persons, of groups, and indeed of nations and ages of history. But especially, inescapably, we determine our own fate. It all happens at a tree that is "in the midst" of our respective gardens.

Well, as Genesis tells it, Adam and Eve couldn't resist the fruit of the tree. "So when the woman saw that the tree was good for food, and that it was a delight to the eyes, and that the tree was to be desired to make one wise, she took of its fruit and ate; and she also gave some to her husband, who was with her, and he ate" (Genesis 3:6). Though it's not the point of the story we're pursuing just now, we should take time to note that Adam and Eve had many good reasons to take the forbidden fruit: it was nourishing, it was aesthetically appealing, and it had uniquely nutritional benefits. There was only one drawback: God had said no, and in taking the fruit, our spiritual ancestors were damaging their relationship to God—and in the process, destroying their own best welfare.

So it was that Adam and Eve moved out of the garden, the place of perfection. As a matter of fact, they were evicted. One hates to admit such a detail in his or her family history, but that's what the record reports. Thus our family story has its most ignominious chapter at the site of a tree. Someone who's looking for an excuse for our human condition might argue that it's all the fault of that tree. Take that tree from the story, and we might still be living in Eden.

But that's just the beginning of our story of trees. Let me move from the tree that is so prominent at the beginning of humanity's spiritual journey to a tree at the climax of our story. We find it in the New Testament book of Revelation. Now we're in a city, not a garden, but it's the kind of city that the greatest city planners have always tried, consciously or not, to replicate. It's a city with an abundance of wealth—gates of pearl and streets of gold—but retaining the wonders of unspoiled nature. A river, "bright as crystal," flows "through the middle of the street of the city," and on either side of the river is (you guessed it) "the tree of life." This tree produces a fruit each month, "and the leaves of the tree are for the healing of the nations. Nothing accursed will be found there any more" (Revelation 22:1-3). Where the tree in Eden was under a shadow of danger, this tree is nothing but blessing. Its supply is monthly, not seasonal, and its fruit with its "healing of the nations" guarantees a world free from strife or poverty or need.

In other words, everything that was lost at the first tree has now been restored, in extravagant abundance, at the new tree: not a single tree at the center of a garden but a symmetry of trees along the banks of a river that wends its way amiably through the city.

You've probably noticed that I've gone from the first tree—a tree of decision, and unfortunately, of trouble—to what appears to be the climaxing tree, a tree of luxurious blessing in the ultimate of our human story. What about the third tree that I promised at the outset of this chapter?

Well, chronologically this tree that I'm talking about third is the second tree, coming at the spiritual midpoint of humankind's history. But because this tree is the most important of all trees, I've saved it for the last. You see, there wouldn't really be a story if it weren't for this tree; or if there were a story, it would be only a tragedy, and ultimate tragedies don't fit with the nature of God. I can't tell you the name of the third tree, nor can I tell you where it grew. I don't know how it looked in its natural state, so I can't tell you if someone ever stood before it and rhapsodized about its beauty. This tree is known for its function, for the service it rendered, however unwillingly. The function was not a noble one. And yet strangely, perhaps even ironically, some of the world's most beautiful songs have celebrated the memory of this tree—and especially for its function. With all the poems that have been written about trees, from scrubs on a hillside to majestic sequoias, I suspect that all of them together haven't been celebrated as much as this one quite ordinary tree.

If you someday visit the land of Israel, your tour guide will take you to two locations where this tree once might have stood. One place is within a quite ornate church, The Church of the Holy Sepulcher, and the other place is a hilltop overlooking a terminal point for city buses in Jerusalem; the former is considered the likely historical spot by many archaeologists and the latter by the sentiment of many travelers. In any event, these are the places where people commemorate a time when some soldiers raised up three crosses for an execution. It was a common scene and a common event in that day; crucifixion was employed by the Roman government to help maintain order in their expanding empire. But this particular execution has found a unique place in history. The crucifixion occurred on a Friday afternoon while people in Jerusalem were trying to finish their business before sundown and the beginning of the Sabbath. As I said, there were three crosses. The two outer crosses held the bodies of two rather well-known local criminals. The center cross was graced by the body of Jesus of Nazareth, the Christ. This was the tree that made history. It is the tree that links the tree in Eden and the tree described in the book of Revelation. Let me tell you what I mean. At the tree in the Garden of Eden, as Genesis tells the story, we humans violated our perfect union with God. In the process, not so incidentally, we also violated our union with one another. Thus the man, Adam, who felt that the woman was the completion of himself, the only thing needed to make Eden truly perfect, decided after the sin at the tree that the woman was the source of his troubles. Still more. What happened at that tree violated something within our own psyche, so that we humans became divided within ourselves. Thus Adam and Eve became embarrassed by themselves, making fig leaves to hide from themselves for as long as the fig leaves might last. And psychologically speaking, they never last long enough.

Now how do we get from the tree in Eden, where we imposed a curse on ourselves, to the eternal city where the tree of life—now in blessed multiples, all along the river— bears constant fruit for the healing of the nations? What is the link?

The link is this tree at Calvary. George Bennard, a preacher and an evangelist in the early twentieth century, described this tree as "so despised by the world," yet confessed in his simple hymn that it had "a wondrous attraction for me."[3] That attraction was not just for Bennard. When one visits a military burial place where no distinctions are given to individual graves, one finds literally acres of plain, white crosses—as if there is no better way to mark death with honor than with this simple tree. People of deep religious commitment often carry a metal or a wooden cross in their pocket, jingling with the commerce of the day, to remind them of whose they are. On my desk, where I write just now, there is a cross shaped (appropriately) out of nails by the skill of a craftsman in Texas. If I go to the finest jewelry store in a street of elite shopping, I will find this tree in astonishing varieties, to wear as a ring, an earring, a pin, a necklace, a bracelet—the possibilities seem almost endless. Such a tree! If it is, as George Bennard said, "so despised by the world," the world shows its despising by embracing the tree widely but with little understanding of its love and its challenge.

By the sacrifice of Jesus our Lord, this tree broke the power of the violation in Eden, and made possible the perfection of the Holy City. Dietrich Bonhoeffer, the German theologian who dared to stand against Hitler and who was hanged on gallows only days before his prison camp was opened by the Allied armies, knew much about the cross by both experience and by his profound theological insight. He wrote, "The only visible sign of God in the world is the cross."[4]

I have pondered Bonhoeffer's words often since first coming upon them. I hear God in so many ways and, in a sense, I see God in so many people and places. But I think I realize what Bonhoeffer was saying: the cross is a visible sign of God. No wonder, then, that we Christians like to raise a cross not only over our church buildings and our rescue missions but also over our hospitals and schools and other institutions. And no wonder, on the other hand, that in some countries of the world believers are forbidden to raise such a marker on house or building—as if the sign of the cross were a threat to the philosophies that dominate such regions.

It *is* a powerful sign, you know; as powerful as we believers allow it to be, as it works its wonders in our lives.

Half a century ago, Jesse Stuart asked himself, as he walked among the familiar trees of his beloved W-Hollow, how all of those trees had been planted. Then he urged his readers, "Walk in a forest of giant trees someday and speculate when and how each tree was planted by Nature's own invisible hand, and whether she employed bird, animal, wind, or rain to assist with her spring planting."[5]

Reading Stuart's words, I asked myself how well we more knowledgeable creatures, we believers, are scattering the seeds of faith, so that the cross will continue to spread its eternal beauty to new places, in future times. This tree, which stands between our separation from God and the ultimate consummation of God's plan: how well are we promoting its growth?

NOTES

1. Walter Russell Bowie, *The Interpreter's Bible,* vol. 1 (Nashville: Abingdon-Cokesbury Press, 1952), 495-96.

2. Robert Frost, *Modern American Poetry,* edited by Louis Untermeyer (New York: Harcourt, Brace and Company, 1942), 229-30.

3. George Bennard, "The Old Rugged Cross," *The United Methodist Hymnal* (Nashville: The United Methodist Publishing House, 1989), 504.

4. Dietrich Bonhoeffer, *I Want to Live These Days with You* (Louisville: Westminster John Knox Press, 2007), 96.

5. Jesse Stuart, *The Year of My Rebirth* (New York: McGraw-Hill Book Company, 1950), 150.

CHAPTER 3

THE NOT-SO-DUMB OX

Scripture Reading: Isaiah 1:1-9

Slang and figures of speech have their seasons, just as necktie and jewelry styles and skirt lengths do. Slang and figures of speech depend on subjects being familiar enough that others will get the point of the language. And the longer the subject is known, the longer the slang or figure of speech lasts. I sometimes wonder if our current generation—or any future one!—will ever produce any language that can truly qualify as slang or a figure of speech because we now live in such different worlds and our interests change so rapidly that no word or idea catches the interest of anything beyond a particular age or social group; and nothing seems to hold the interest of our culture for more than a month or six weeks.

It wasn't always this way. There was a time when a slang phrase, a clever saying, a figure of speech captured a whole nation—and indeed, in some cases was translated into other languages. And there was a time when such phrases passed on from generation to generation, because the subject was familiar to each passing generation.

I'm thinking of that kind of phrase just now. It was still used familiarly (though rather unpleasantly) when I was a boy. We know it was used in Shakespeare's day, as I shall explain in a moment. And the Scripture passage I want to talk about demonstrates that the idea, if not the actual phrase, was common in biblical times, at least 2,600 years ago. It's a bit of slang that lived on because it was part of a world that was unchanged for thousands of years, the world of agriculture, a world that depended upon beasts of burden—a world where the ox was part of everyone's day.

Oxen are, in their own way, remarkable creatures. We don't see much of them in our part of the world, not even in farming communities, but they are still an essential part of agriculture in most of the world. An encyclopedia will tell you that they have heavy bodies, long tails, and divided hoofs, and that they chew the cud. Their heavy bodies equip them to pull great loads, and their long tails effectively drive away pesky insects. If ever an animal could be called a beast of burden, it is the ox. And although in its wild state—as with the undomesticated water buffalo or the yak or the musk ox—it can be quite a fierce animal, in its domesticated state, in an un-motorized world, it well may be the farmer's best friend.

And because the domestic ox does its job without complaint, rarely resisting, quietly obeying orders, it has found its place in slang. Unkind, abusive slang! As I said earlier, Shakespeare made the reference in his play *The Merry Wives of Windsor*. When Falstaff said, "I do perceive that I am made an ass," Ford replied, "Aye, and an ox, too." It was a common phrase in my Iowa boyhood, even in city life. Someone who seemed slow to get a point was likely to be told that he was "a dumb ox."

Obviously, the figure of speech was common in the days of the prophet Isaiah, some six hundred years before Jesus was born. The prophet was making an appeal to God's people, the Jews, to remember the place God ought to have in their lives. Isaiah's feelings on the matter were so strong that he called upon heaven and earth to hear what he had to say. Then, having commandeered the universe for his audience, Isaiah spoke these words on God's behalf:

I reared children and brought them up,
> but they have rebelled against me.
The ox knows its owner,
> and the donkey its master's crib;
but Israel does not know,
> my people do not understand. (Isaiah 1:2-3)

Dumb ox? Yes, in some ways. The ox doesn't understand calculus and can't operate a computer and doesn't carry a Blackberry. The ox doesn't know the calorie count in a bagel or the difference between a simile and a metaphor. In fact, there are a great many things an ox doesn't know! But the ox has this premier intelligence: it knows where *home* is. It knows the voice of its owner. So the ox may not be so dumb after all. It knows the most important, most basic issues of its own existence, its own daily welfare and survival.

We humans are likely to dismiss the ox's conduct as "just animal instinct." But here's an interesting matter. When Isaiah said that the ox "knows" its owner, he used a Hebrew word that means "coming to know through association." That's the process through which the ox passes. The animal works with a farmer, is fed by him, is perhaps beaten and certainly corrected by him, then through these accumulated experiences, the ox comes to know its master. In time and by experience, the ox responds to its owner's voice and commands as to no other.

It is at this point that the prophet Isaiah made his comparison between the ox and the prophet's people, the nation of Israel: "but Israel does not know, / my people do not understand." The ox and the donkey, poor beasts of burden, seem wiser than this enlightened people, this nation that has been blessed with centuries of sustained relationship with the Lord God.

We humans are different from the ox because we have the ability to reason. We take our experiences and put them into a thinking process. But our reasoning is not pure or mechanical; it isn't like a computer. Emotional elements enter into our reasoning, and moral elements, and peculiar factors of prejudice—some of them so deeply hidden that we don't recognize their existence. Specifically, we take our remarkable ability to reason and introduce into it the ability to rationalize. This is a neat trick! We use our reasoning powers not necessarily to fulfill our responsibilities but to evade them—and even to justify ourselves as we do so. Let's examine the matter at some very simple, everyday levels. For instance, take a speed limit. Reason says that we should obey it, because the law has been instituted for our own safety and that of others. Do we do so? Not necessarily; we may use our clever minds to determine where we can disobey this law and yet not get a fine. Or consider matters of health. Studies show that drinking alcohol or using tobacco or overeating will harm our bodies. Since you and I are reasoning creatures, we should need no further incentive: we have the knowledge of our physician and a cadre of research specialists. Do we follow their counsel? Not necessarily; we may choose instead to argue with the data and to rationalize our way around the facts. Sometimes, even the physicians and researchers who provide us with the data find themselves ignoring it.

It's especially interesting to see how carefully we adapt our knowledge to suit our purposes. For instance, the television industry insists that its programs do not affect the lives of its viewers, and that the conduct of children or young people is not shaped in any way by portrayals of violence or crude conduct on television. But then the industry tells its potential advertisers that portraying their products on television will persuade people to purchase those products. If only the ox could speak, it would be interesting to see what the "dumb ox" would say about such reasoning.

So it is that some twenty-six centuries ago God explained through the prophet Isaiah that the people didn't *know,* didn't *understand.* "The ox knows its owner, the donkey its master's crib, but...my people do not understand."

You see, God expects us to understand. God, who has provided us with the instruments of intelligence, memory, and reason, with the ability to comprehend—God expects us to use these instruments to our benefit, especially the eternal benefit to be found in our relationship with God. We can't be easily excused for failing to use the gifts with which God has empowered us.

God pays us the supreme compliment of offering to talk things over. Thus the prophet Isaiah continues his appeal to the people:

> Come now, let us argue it out,
>   says the LORD:
> though your sins are like scarlet,
>   they shall be like snow;
> though they are red like crimson,
>   they shall become like wool. (Isaiah 1:18)

God is willing to "argue" with us, to talk things over. God honors our capacity for reason by seeking to reason with us. Consider in this offer both the extraordinary humility of God, and the exceeding compliment God pays to our humanness.

But the reasoning God seeks is of a very special kind. If I were speaking philosophically, I think I might call it *existential* reasoning. I choose, rather, to call it *family* reasoning because God so often describes Israel—and by extension, all believers—in family terms, such as sons and daughters, or spouses. That is, the reasoning that is involved in Isaiah's appeal is the kind of reasoning that occurs within relationships.

We usually think of reason as a cold, detached state. We may picture someone laying out a logical argument in one-two-three fashion, an argument that leads to a conclusion beyond further discussion. "That's reasonable," we say, and that's the end of it. But even reason depends on its setting.

Some matters can be concluded at a calculating machine or the figure at the end of a series of numbers or symbols.

But there's more to reason than that. So it is that a wise man—a very wise man!—wrote, "The heart has its reasons which reason does not know."[1] If a poet had said that, or if you found it in a romantic novel (where, no doubt, it has been quoted scores of times), you might discredit it. The statement comes, however, from Blaise Pascal (1623–1662), the French scientist, philosopher, and mathematician, one of the few true geniuses in human history, a person whose discoveries paved the way for the calculating machine. But with all of the penetrating power of Pascal's mathematical genius, there was a place in his soul for a deeper kind of reason, the reason that comes from a relationship. Pascal found this relationship with God. During a November night in 1654, Pascal experienced God in a way that he said was "not of philosophers and men of science," but which nevertheless left him with "Certainty. Certainty. Feeling of Joy and Peace. The God of Jesus Christ.... Joy, Joy, Joy, Tears of Joy." Pascal sewed a written copy of his experience into the lining of his clothes, to be carried with him until his death. The great logician had his reasons, reasons that had come from a relationship.

Pascal knew this from his relationship with God, which is my primary point just now. But all of us know something about the reason of relationship from common experiences. When a parent and a child reason with one another, the process is different from a syllogism on paper, because when parent and child talk together, they're not simply dealing with abstract issues but also with shared experiences and memories: indeed, with blood and heartbeat, tears and laughter. Thus in a conversation between longtime friends, the "facts" of a matter are seen through the prism of shared loyalties and common dreams of years yet to come.

Jesus reasoned from relationships when he discussed religion with the key religious leaders of his day, the scribes and Pharisees. They were good and earnest men, but they tended to see life primarily through measurable laws. Thus when they saw Jesus heal a man on the Sabbath day, they could understand only that a law had been broken. But Jesus reasoned that life is like the relationship of a father and a son, so he told the story of a young man who left home and who humiliated his father by his conduct, but when the young man returned home, his father forgave him and restored the father-son relationship.

That's the point the prophet Isaiah was making. He told his generation, "You think the donkey is a ridiculous creature and the ox is stupid, but they're smart enough to know *home*; they recognize their master's crib, the place of their daily sustenance. What's wrong with you, that you don't know *home,* don't understand where your proper existence lies?" Many scholars feel that these paragraphs at the very beginning of the book of Isaiah were probably written after the rest of the book was complete, and that the prophet meant them to be a preface to all that followed. This section is a summary of the whole burden of the prophet. The ox knows home; why don't we?

Another great Hebrew prophet, Hosea, preached some years before Isaiah, but he made the same kind of appeal. His point of reference was not that of ox and owner but of child and parent. When Israel was a child, Hosea said, God loved him and called him, like a son, out of Egypt. "I . . . taught [them] to walk," God said, "took them up in my arms; but they did not know that I healed them" (Hosea 11:1, 3). Again, that sad, melancholy phrase: "they did not know."

And what would God say to you, to me? For some, "I knew you as a child, when you prayed at night to be protected from the dark. I loved you even before you lisped, 'Now I lay me down to sleep.' I remembered you when you lied to your teacher, then cried at the thought of it as you ran home after school. I held you in my arms during your appendectomy. How can you forget me now?"

Some hear a voice from a later but equally poignant memory. "You knew I was with you in your lonely military patrol; how come you've forgotten me now?" And a voice that recalls no moving drama but that gets its authenticity from the years of time and from the peculiar grandeur of commonness: "You were my child in the church school. I spoke to you so often during a hymn or a choir anthem, or the singing of a favorite chorus." And again, "Remember how you prayed after the exploratory surgery, and the tearful gratitude you felt when the doctor said there was no malignancy? How is it that you have forgotten me now?"

There's no end, I suspect, to the scenes you and I can call up from memory if we will. They have their various degrees of emotion, of once-in-a-lifetime or of daily commonness, but they are the voices of *reason,* the special kind of reason that comes from relationships. And what bothered the prophet Isaiah—and what continues to bother you and me in our best, rational moments—is our propensity for being unreasonable. We look at the dumb ox, a dull, plodding creature so easily scorned and turned into a figure of speech. But this ox *knows* his master! How is it that you and I, so admirably equipped with memory and reason, don't know, don't understand? How is it that we forget what we ought most to remember and that we reason in such shallow fashion?

Perhaps the ox isn't so dumb after all. Perhaps we could learn from the ox: we could come to *know,* and to *understand.* Perhaps, if we allowed our reasoning to be more reasonable.

NOTE

1. Pascal, *Pensees,* 277.

CHAPTER 4

FASHION SHOW IN A FIELD

Scripture Reading: Matthew 6:25-34

What world event would bring more than a thousand newspaper and magazine writers to Paris at one time? Perhaps a meeting of some major committee of the United Nations? Or perhaps the possibility of an announcement of a landmark medical discovery, something that will stop the scourge of a dreaded, deadly illness? It's possible that you are enough of a student of human nature and of economics that you already know better. Before I can tell you, you may have guessed that this massive gathering of journalists from all over the world come to Paris annually for the revealing of the new fashions in clothing. And with them will come more than five thousand retailers, ready to follow through on the buzz of excitement or rejection that this gathering will bring.

Nearly twenty centuries ago, Jesus asked a group of people who had settled on a hillside in order to hear him teach, "Why do you worry about clothing?" (Matthew 6:28). I wonder what Jesus would say today, if he were to arrive in Paris along with this breathless throng. And I wonder still more how this gathering—so sophisticated in taste, so enraptured with fashion—would respond to Jesus' question. And I wonder how the newspaper, magazine, and television reporters would handle Jesus. I suspect they would find him rather quaint. Some able columnist with a knack for human interest writing would enjoy explaining to his or her readers about this unusual man whose outlook was so contrary to the mood of the café and lounge crowd.

But before I go any further, let me say that I have nothing against looking nice. Whether you believe it or not, I try hard, personally, to look as good as I can (and the older I get, the more effort it takes). I'm in favor of beauty. I like for things—and for people—to be as beautiful as possible. Indeed, this is part of the point of everything I hope to say in the next several pages. I'm for beauty: for you, for me, for everybody. I'd rather look at lovely things than at distasteful ones, and I honor anyone who hopes to make himself or herself easier to look at. With that understood, let me hurry on.

If you had been present on that long-ago day when Jesus said, "Why do you worry about clothing?" you most likely would have said, "These people have good reason to worry!" Their garments were simple in the extreme; *basic* is probably the kindest word. On their feet, they wore a pair of sandals, sturdy but with no distinguishing lines and no evidence of designer influence. Covering the body was a loose robe, if you could call it that; for the common folk, it was a garment so simple they could wear it by day and use it for a blanket by night. Their undergarments were equally simple. In other words, if they worried about clothing, their worry was primarily about having enough to cover the body. We worry about being fashionable; they worried about keeping warm on cool days, or at the least, modestly covered.

Nevertheless, I submit that they were conscious of fashion. You don't have to have the money to buy expensive clothes to recognize that such clothing exists. What we might call the "better classes," especially among the Romans, wore garments which distinguished them from the masses. Without a doubt, most people dreamed of a day when they or their children might be able to look wealthy, glamorous, sophisticated—whatever the goals may have been in that no-doubt simpler time.

So Jesus said to such a gathering, "Why do you worry about clothing? Consider the lilies of the field, how they grow; they neither toil nor spin, yet I tell you, even Solomon in all his glory was not clothed like one of these" (Matthew 6:28-29).

Jesus was inviting his listeners to attend a fashion show in a field! Can you imagine the thousand journalists and five thousand buyers hurrying to a *field*? Not an English garden, not a greenhouse or a terraced park, but just a field. And not to see the exotic displays you might find in the celebrated rose garden in Shreveport, Louisiana, or the annual spring event in some of the Dutch settlements in America's Midwest, but just lilies of the field, a display that might be attended almost any day in season.

The flower Jesus referred to was a common flower, wild in any field—scarlet poppies and anemones, the windflower. They carpeted the hillside each year after the early rain, growing all along the roadside, ranging in color from glowing crimson to a brilliant purple. They required no cultivation, no skilled care or fertilizer. They were as common in Jesus' world as dandelions are in ours—and as you know, that which is common generally is not prized. Besides, although they were brilliant in color, they lasted hardly a day. Then, women in the first century world would gather the dried plants to make a quick fire, to heat up the cooking ovens. These flowers had only one day of life, yet for that day, they were blessed with a beauty which we human beings cannot successfully duplicate. It is as if they were nature's careless throwaway.

Since Jesus was preaching outdoors, his point must have been very dramatic. Imagine him on a hillside, saying, "Why do you worry about your clothing?"—then, pointing a bare stone's throw away: "Look at those flowers! When King Solomon was at his greatest, his designers couldn't produce an outfit like that. Yet before this day is over, some of you will stuff them in your oven to get ready for your evening meal."

Those lilies had a secret: they were beautiful, and they didn't worry about it. God had made them beautiful, and they simply let God's original provisions shine through. You and I start off as well as the lilies, but we have a hard time following through. God made us beautiful too. Every one of us. In spite of some feature we wish we hadn't inherited from the "wrong side" of the family, or much worse, the tendency toward grumpiness we got from another, we're still beautiful as we enter this world. We enter the world full of potential, and we're unique. True, we're in need of redemption; we need to be born again. But we're full of potential for the purposes of God and of our own conquest of life.

But back to the lilies. Their beauty is on the outside where everyone can see it, but it comes from the inside. You never see a flower primping itself; it isn't necessary to gild the lily! The lily draws its beauty from the soil, in which it has its roots, and from its own inherent capacity as a lily. We human beings, by contrast, keep working on the outside. I think of a woman (it could as well have been a man, but in this instance it was a woman) who had obviously gone to great effort to make herself attractive. She had invested substantially in coiffure and manicure, and her fashion, from the cut of her shoes to her choice of dress, was in exquisite taste. Her face was exquisitely made up. Unfortunately, she had forgotten one thing. She hadn't taken care of her interior, and this reflected itself in her face. Her facial expression was somewhere between unpleasant and condescending. Cosmetics couldn't do a thing to remedy that.

I'm sure the woman would have been unbelieving if she knew it, but I felt quite sorry for her. It was really very sad to see someone go to such expense and such an investment in time to make a favorable impression, only to forget something which wouldn't have cost her a cent: a pleasant, loving attitude.

But here's the irony of the matter, you see. Our beauty

treatments—those things we put on from the outside—are so likely, by nature, to be self-defeating. They tend to be self-centered, in which case, they do bad things to the face. By contrast, if we try to make ourselves look nice for the pleasure of other people—a friend, or a spouse, or perhaps our children or a parent—we escape this hazard. But to the degree that our beauty treatments are self-centered, seeking simply to bring attention to ourselves or to impress others, they are self-defeating.

The lily is unself-conscious. It isn't thinking about itself. It's just doing its thing, being God's lily.

When we're born, we get the face and form that are delivered to us by nature, via our family heritage. Sometimes nature seems to play bizarre tricks in the way it reaches back among our ancestors to present us with a certain nose, a particular twinkle in the eye, a texture of hair. Sometimes family members tell us from whom we "got" particular characteristics, including personality traits. But as time goes by, we begin to get the face and the temperament we make for ourselves. Elbert Hubbard, that disarmingly wise philosopher who was so popular in another generation, once said something like this: "Beauty not only leaves some faces, it leaves behind a record as to where it has gone." If you want to test Hubbard's thinking, live long enough to attend your fiftieth class reunion. The twenty-fifth will give you a start, but it takes the fiftieth to bring our human efforts to full development.

It's quite an amazing experience. It has only a little to do with weight and dress and almost everything with what people have had on their minds for the past fifty years. It can be disillusioning to see what has happened to the cheerleader you adored from a distance or the big man on campus who now looks like someone from whom you wouldn't want to buy your pension program. Where did the teenage beauty go, or the arresting handsomeness? It was taken over by self-centered living, by worry, by thoughts of revenge and resentment. Hateful words, both spoken and heard, have left their lines in the face, and fear has left its imprint too. A fellow said one day, when he looked at an old pick-up truck in a parking lot, "That truck has seen a lot of back-country roads." I think of that sometimes, when I see some faces, sometimes of people still in their forties. Mind you, sometimes folks aren't to be blamed singularly for the face they've gotten, because it hasn't been a solo job. Some people get pretty well worked over by people around them, and some of us are fortunate in having been blessed by friends and family who have brought out the best in us.

And of course, it's by no means a matter of what happens to us. Rather, it's what we do with what happens to us. And here again is a lesson from the flowers of the field. They keep their beauty no matter where they are. Years ago, a train on which I was traveling stopped in a small station on the edge of an industrial center. It was a generally ugly spot, but in the midst of the gravel and concrete weariness, some flowers were growing. No one had planted them; they had simply asserted themselves in spite of the environment. They were doing their thing, just being flowers. And that means being beautiful wherever you are.

And how often they add beauty where otherwise none would appear! New York City's potter's field has been the subject of many articles; I have read such in newspapers in both New York and London. They tell of the starkness of this place where so many hundreds of thousands of unclaimed bodies have been buried since 1845. But in the midst of the weeds that grow like a jungle, one reporter noted the bright blue cornflowers. Flowers do that. They grow wild, even in places that, philosophically speaking, reject them. That remarkable seventeenth-century pastor-poet, George Herbert, said, "And here in dust and dirt, O here / The lilies of [God's] love appear."

Mary Lou Carney could offer her own interpretation of Herbert's lines. When she saw her sister planting flowers one day, Carney asked where she'd gotten them. In the dump, her sister said. One of the major growers in her city threw away any plant that didn't measure up to its demanding standards. Now, several years later, Carney marvels at the luxurious roses that grace her sister's yard, remembering that they had been "picked from the trash." Now, she says, they're "offering their beauty to everyone who sees."[1] I see them as kin to Jesus' lilies of the field, still operating on the same principle two thousand years later. And I venture that it's because flowers find their roots in God's sustaining love. This gives them the character to rise above any ugliness around them. So, too, with us, if we will. But we, too, will succeed in such beauty and such endurance only if we keep our roots in God.

But if the flowers have an edge on us, it is this, that their beauty comes naturally, while ours, as time goes by, must be chosen. By the same token, you and I have an edge on the flowers. For the flowers eventually wither and die. But if we will clothe ourselves in God's love, we will—in the truest sense—only get better. In the course of the last twenty years, I have preached in several hundred churches. In every instance, I have come upon lovely human beings who have been working on their faces for a long time, generally without knowing they were doing so. Now, growing older, they are beautiful, with that beauty which simply cannot be gotten at age twenty and which surely can't be gotten at a spa or at the cosmetics counter.

And I apologize again for what may seem like an attack on physical attractiveness or for our efforts to make ourselves physically attractive. As I said earlier, I'm grateful for beauty, wherever it appears. I am glad for every attempt to make the world more beautiful, whether it is by beautiful faces, well-chosen clothing, fine architecture, or clean streets. But I mean to raise a question about the way we hope to bring beauty into our world.

Because, you see, the best of beauty can't really be purchased. The beauty that matters most comes through a quality of life. When it is a matter of the human face, there is a winsomeness that can't be gotten by toiling or spinning, as Jesus said, but by immersing ourselves in the grace of God and in wholesome living.

When Jesus spoke that day on a Palestinian hillside and asked, "Why do you worry about clothing?" he wasn't giving helpful hints on how to put together a winning wardrobe. His theme was trust in God: Don't worry yourself to death, Jesus was saying; remember that God takes care of the birds of the air and the lilies of the field, and God will watch over us, too, to the degree that we'll allow him to do so.

But there's a second lesson, too, because Jesus was talking indirectly about beauty. He was reminding us that the lilies had a secret of loveliness, and that if we're wise, we'll learn from them. Because deep-down, real loveliness and abiding beauty can't be found in the pages of *Vogue* or of *GQ,* or in the windows of Neiman Marcus, Saks Fifth Avenue, or Nordstrom's. The secret, if we will attend to it, is in that fashion show in the field, where God spreads beauty with prodigal pleasure. Look at it! Even the fashion models in Paris aren't arrayed like these! It is a beauty that God makes available to anyone who wants it. It comes without money and without price. It is the gift of grace, distributed as we live our lives with gratitude, with kindness toward all, with trust in God, and with more attention to others than to self. It is the life of love and commitment, and beauty is its natural by-product.

NOTE

1. Mary Lou Carney, *Daily Guideposts, 2008* (Carmel, N.Y.: Guideposts, 2007), 143-44.

CHAPTER 5

A GOOD WORD FOR
THE SPIDER

Scripture Reading: Proverbs 30:24-28

Thomas DeWitt Talmage was one of America's best
known preachers in the latter half of the nineteenth
century, serving pulpits consecutively in Philadelphia,
Brooklyn, and Washington, D.C. His oratory often swept
to imaginative heights, so his congregation in Brooklyn was
probably not surprised when he began a sermon one Sunday, "We are all watching for phenomena. A sky full of stars
shining from January to January calls out not so many remarks as the blazing of one meteor."

But I'm sure not many were ready a few minutes later
when he continued, "You may take your telescope and
sweep it across the heavens in order to behold the glory of
God; but I shall take the leaf holding the spider and the spider's web, and I shall bring the microscope to my eye, and
while I gaze and look, and study, and am confounded, I will
kneel down in the grass and cry: 'Great and marvelous are
Thy works, Lord God Almighty!'"[1]

His sermon was not a flight of fancy. Dr. Talmage had
a text, and it was a legitimate one: Proverbs 30:28 (KJV)—
"The spider taketh hold with her hands, and is in
kings' palaces." The New Revised Standard Version chooses
to replace "spider" with "lizard" in its translation, but

acknowledges in a footnote that spider is an equally correct translation, so Talmage has lost nothing in the passing of a century or more.

But before I go further, I must confess that I follow this great preacher of the past with some reluctance. I've never been high on spiders. When one appears in our home, Janet carefully picks it up with a facial tissue and carries it outdoors, feeling it got into our house by mistake. I admire her concern for living things, and I agree with her philosophically, but spiders still don't really appeal to me.

Nevertheless, I know that Dr. Talmage was right, and of course, I agree with that wise man long ago, Agur, who gave us the thirtieth chapter of Proverbs. He wrote, "Four things on earth are small, / yet they are exceedingly wise," and took for his examples the ant, the badger, the locust, and the spider.

So let me tell you about the spider. This little creature isn't as appealing as the stars on a cloudless night or the breeze that plays with the leaves outside my window at this moment as I write. But the spider is part of God's creation, and perhaps all the more wonderful for being so small, so intricate, and so lacking in attractive features—unless, of course, you are a student of spiders.

This eight-legged creature can be smaller than the head of a pin or as large as a man's hand. Some live below water, while others live near the top of Mount Everest. All spiders spin silk, all have fangs, and most have poison glands, although only a few are dangerous to humans. There are more than 29,000 known kinds of spiders, but scientists estimate that their variety may reach 50,000 or more.

Spiders eat only liquids, sucking the body fluids of their catch. But the spider can eat some of the solid material by spraying digestive juices, which dissolve the tissue and leave the fluids. This is how a tarantula can eat a mouse, though it takes roughly a day and a half for the predigestive juices to reduce the mouse to a bit of hair and bones.

But was the wise man exaggerating when he included

spiders among the creatures that he considered "exceedingly wise"? Jesse Stuart, the remarkable novelist and poet, grew up very close to nature in Greenup County, Kentucky. In one of his books, he tells of an April morning when he was thinking of setting out strawberry plants, until a neighbor, Glen Hilton, told him it was the wrong day to do so. Hilton pointed to the bluffs, bottoms, and flats—spiderwebs everywhere.

Stuart, a better-than-average student of nature himself, asked, "What do the spiderwebs have to do with setting the strawberry plants?"

"There's coming a long dry spell," Hilton replied. "I have never seen it fail."

Stuart countered, "But look at the overcast. It will be raining before this afternoon."

Hilton was unmoved. "No, it won't. No, it won't rain. The spiders know. The spiders are always right. You'll see."

Later that morning the overcast had disappeared, the sun was high in a blue sky, and the dew had dried from the spiderwebs. Jesse Stuart comments to the readers, "I wondered who told the spiders."[2]

A remarkable little creature, the spider. Not only can it find its way into kings' palaces, while others dream of an invitation, it knows when the rain is coming—knows even better than the farmer who has studied the sky for years.

Somewhere once, I read the story of a devout Catholic monk who was a premier mathematician. One day while waiting upon God in his morning meditations, he noticed a spider weaving its web in a corner of his small room. For days, that spider and its web became the subject of the monk's meditation. As a mathematician and an engineer, he saw the intricate interweaving and structuring that made the slender threads of silk strong enough to catch and hold a flying creature, food for the spider's sustenance.

In what technical school was the spider trained? Who was her professor of structural engineering? With what instruments did she measure the tensile strength of her silk?

How did she learn to take up residence in a king's palace—
or in this instance, in a monk's cell? If one is a thorough-
going evolutionist who leaves no room for God in the
creative process, it is no wonder that one must consider
millions of years to see such skills develop in one of nature's
lowliest creatures, a tiny thing (usually) that can be wiped
out with a swat or a step. And if, on the other hand, one
places God at the heart of creation, one pictures a God who
delights in detail to such a degree that even a spider is a
work of art.

I confess, nevertheless, that I don't enjoy spiders. I suppose that the spider is, for me, like certain rooms in an art
gallery: I know that genius is on display, but not the type of
genius that I want to dwell upon. But like that wise man,
Agur, I am in awe of these "things on earth [that] are small,
/ yet they are exceedingly wise" (Proverbs 30:24).

Those wise folks of old measured wisdom largely on
the creature's ability to survive. It was the same kind of
pragmatism that made the writer of Ecclesiastes reason that
"a living dog is better than a dead lion" (Ecclesiastes 9:4). So
while I marvel at the spider, and while with DeWitt Talmage I will see the wonders of God's creation in the spider
as well as in the unfathomed heavens, the spider has a quite
limited place in my book of life's lessons.

I venture that no one in the spider's world ever asks,
"What would you be if you couldn't be a building engineer,
specializing in buildings that catch food?" Nor does anyone
ever say to a spider in its time of adolescence, "What do you
hope to be when you grow up?" And this is because all of the
spider's intricate skills lead to one end—food for survival.
The spider doesn't dream of a life that will also include time
to read a book or to listen to a symphony. It is enough that
the spider's web will collect food for another period of time.
Meanwhile, the spider cares not at all that a biblical writer
twenty-five or more centuries ago praised its skills, or that
scientists study it, or that E. B. White imagined a member of

its clan so wise and compassionate that millions of children and adults are delighted to be caught in *Charlotte's Web*.

All of which makes one ask some serious questions about spiders and humans. As far as we can see, the spider has one calling in life. It is not to be an engineer, in spite of its unique gift for building suspension structures. And although spiders perform a valuable service to us humans by catching millions of flies and other insects, I don't think the spider knows the value of his services, nor does he rejoice at the end of the day in the good he has performed for the human race. Come to think of it, we rarely thank him for this service, so we can't blame the spider for not recognizing his value to us.

But if somehow the spider could comprehend how important he is in our human equation, I'm quite sure he wouldn't work any more earnestly at his task. Because, of course, he's catching these little critters for only one purpose, a very basic one: they are his means of survival, his daily bread, if you please. He works to live. He doesn't work to get ahead, to build up a pension for retirement, to get an education for his offspring, or to give to the Charity for Indigent Spiders. He catches flies so he can live another day to catch more flies. Ad infinitum, until he reaches old age or until some other predatory creature catches him or until some human steps on him.

At this point, some sensitive person might say to himself or herself, "I know *people* like that. They work just to make a living. Week after week, year after year. That's all they get out of life: they just work, eat, sleep and get up to work again, just keeping one step ahead of their creditors."

That's very sad, but let me tell you something equally sad, perhaps even sadder. Jesus told a story about a successful farmer-businessman. He was so successful—partly, I imagine, because of the bountiful blessings of nature in a good crop, and partly because of his astute management—that he found he didn't have enough storage capacity for his harvest. Quite logically he reasoned, "I will pull down my barns and build larger ones." In truth, he was quite a modern sort; you may have met him at your country club, or he may be your next-door neighbor. "And I will say to my soul, Soul, you have ample goods laid up for many years; relax, eat, drink, be merry." But Jesus called him a *fool,* a word Jesus said we should use sparingly if at all. This man was a fool, Jesus said, because he didn't recognize that on that "very night" his life would be demanded of him (Luke 12:13-21).

I think Jesus was saying that the man had himself confused with a spider. A spider works only to survive, to meet its physical needs. But there's more to us humans. We are accountable to almighty God. Someday, we have to report to our Creator about what we've done with our lives. And while the Bible recommends careful use of our money and our other resources, God won't be satisfied that we've built larger barns—or a greater accumulation of mutual funds and real estate.

Sometimes when I'm driving through the beautiful countryside, I have an unpleasant thought. Perhaps I should ask forgiveness for it, but hear me. I see the cattle grazing and realize that this is their life, all day long. They are grazing creatures, these cattle. Their time is spent filling their digestive systems. Humans make use of the results, in dairy products or in beef, but this is not by the intention of the cattle; their nature is simply to graze. Then I ask myself how many people are grazing creatures, living simply for what they can put into themselves. The more fortunate have an edge on the cattle because they can choose their field. Some even become connoisseurs; they learn the better grains, so to speak, and they refine their tastes—but still, they live only for what they can pour into themselves. Some become heavy and some sleek (I speak not simply of their physical appearance but of their total person), but still, all that they have is turned in upon themselves.

A vigorous voice in my soul insists that God intended you and me to be more than grazing animals. We are creatures with judgment. We can decide how we invest not only our money but more particularly our talent, and most especially our time. We can decide if everything we have—our energy, our time, our ability, and our resources—will be turned simply to our own passing pleasure and benefit, or whether we will seek to give something of ourselves to others.

I believe that God is satisfied with grazing animals and spiders when they use their particular skills to stay alive and to fulfill their place in the economy of the planet. But I believe that God is not satisfied when we humans do no better than the grazing animal or the spider. Equipped as we are with judgment, with some measure of self-perception, and with the capacity to see the needs of the world around us—and from that seeing, to recognize how we might help meet the need—we then are expected by God to make use of what we are given.

Another word about the spider and the human. As far as we know, no spider dies feeling unfulfilled. The spider does its instinctive, quite impressive thing, using the equipment which nature has provided. But I worry about those humans who never have an opportunity to fulfill their capacity or even to discover that they have such a capacity. I still thank God for the day my seventh-grade English teacher told me that I had been chosen to take Latin, if I wished to do so. I thank God for the grade-school teachers who had sharpened my skills so that I was qualified for this selection. And I thank God that my parents, though having no more than an eighth-grade education themselves, agreed that I should accept the chance to take Latin.

But then I think of all those students whose potential might have been greater than mine but who somehow didn't have the encouragement of a perceptive teacher, or if they brought home the invitation to take an advanced class, were told by their parents that it would be a waste of time. I'm always asking myself how many potential artists, administrators, teachers, poets, research scientists, surgeons, or preachers have been compelled by neglect to live far below the potential God has invested in their lives. And still another word. We humans have a soul. As I have already indicated, I am quite astonished by the skills God has invested in a spider. I marvel at the spider's built-in factory that can produce silk thread, and at the spider's engineering gifts, so that it can find a suitable location and build its little business. And more than that, as Jesse Stuart learned, the spider is so sensitive to its environment that it knows when and when not to go into business!

But the spider doesn't ask, "What is your will for me, almighty God?" And the spider doesn't write a psalm in praise to God, nor does it shape its conduct according to what it perceives God might want of it.

So I say a good word for the spider. I agree with the wise man so long ago: though small, the spider finds its way into the king's palace. And the spider takes care of itself, with equipment that quite baffles me. But the spider never struggles with the choice between good and evil, or the more complicated choice between the good and the best. And the spider never feels the call of God to reach out beyond itself and to bless the world. The spider never wonders how God will judge its days upon this earth. We humans bear the burden of questions and struggles of the soul. And it is that burden that fills the soul with awe and eternity. Awe at the wonders of life and creation, including the spider. And gratitude that we have the capacity for eternity.

NOTES

1. T. DeWitt Talmage, "The Spider in Palaces," *20 Centuries of Great Preaching,* Vol. V (Waco, Tex.: Word Books, 1971), 301, 303.

2. Jesse Stuart, *The Year of My Rebirth* (New York: McGraw-Hill Book Company, 1956), 100-101.

CHAPTER 6

WHEN THE TREES HELD
AN ELECTION

Scripture Reading: Judges 9:8-15

D o trees think? And if they do, do they converse with one another? We have learned that birds communicate. From what ornithologists have been able thus far to discover, birds talk primarily about sources of food and matters of survival. Perhaps some day, we'll discover that bushes and trees and grasses have some method of communication as well. A great biblical poet anticipated a day when the nations of earth will recognize the Lord as king, and when that happens, he said, "Then shall all the trees of the forest sing for joy" (Psalm 96:12). I understand why the psalmist wrote that way, because I have the same feeling of trees singing for joy some mornings when I look out the window of my study. The prophet Isaiah predicted a time when the will of God will be done throughout the world; when that happens, Isaiah said, "all the trees of the field shall clap their hands" (Isaiah 55:12). That's a lovely scene: trees clapping their hands in celebration for what is happening on our planet. I'd love to see it as well as imagine it.

Poets and prophets talk that way because they see life with a kind of wholeness that the rest of us rarely grasp. You and I thought that way, too, when we were children. That's why we loved the stories of Peter Rabbit or Pooh

Bear and Eeyore, or the rollicking good fun Edward Lear imagined when an Owl and a Pussy-Cat "went to sea / In a beautiful pea-green boat."

Mind you, I'm not really so interested in what science may someday discover about the way the several elements of nature communicate with one another, or even if they do. I'm simply reflecting on the fact that at our best—that is, at our most childlike and therefore most imaginative— we humans learn some things best when we can put them into nature stories; that is, when we let bears become philosophers and allow rabbits to become wiser than Farmer Brown.

I say all of this to introduce you to a Bible story that I'm rather sure you've never noticed. It's brief, but it is significant. And I dare to venture that it has something frightfully vital to say to those of us who live in a political system that seeks to practice democracy. Or for that matter, in almost any other political system, because we humans are always involved in forms of government that structure and control our lives.

You'll find my story in the Old Testament book of Judges. This book tells the story of the nation of Israel, when its nationhood was very perilously structured. As the writer says in the closing sentence of the book and once before, those were days when "there was no king in Israel; all the people did what was right in their own eyes" (Judges 21:25). The stories in this book are sometimes wild and always rather wonderful, but I'd rather read about them than to live in their kind of confusion.

This story began in the days of a judge named Gideon. God called Gideon when the nation of Israel was oppressed by their neighbors, the Midianites. The Midianites so dominated Israel that they would "destroy the produce of the land . . . and leave no sustenance in Israel, and no sheep or ox or donkey. . . . Thus Israel was greatly impoverished because of Midian; and the Israelites cried out to the LORD for help" (Judges 6:4-6).

Gideon didn't seem a likely hero at such a time. When the angel of the Lord called him, Gideon answered, "My clan is the weakest in Manasseh [a tribe of Israel], and I am the least in my family" (Judges 6:15). I can't say for sure that his clan really was the weakest (that's a pretty large negative claim), or that Gideon was the least in the lot, but since he was using that data to excuse himself from action, it's clear that he wasn't the kind of strong, vigorous leader a nation in despair would seek out.

But God used him, nevertheless. This is not uncommon in the Scriptures. God seems often to specialize in unlikely people, a fact that should humble any of us who identify ourselves as being called by God. Gideon succeeded so well that he ruled over Israel for forty years, a period marked by peace once the Midianites were subdued.

Gideon seemed to enjoy the fruits of his success. It's interesting to see the way we humans become accustomed to a way of life that we once could not even have imagined. In Gideon's case, living as he did in a quite different world where success was often measured more in family than in possessions, he "had many wives," and from them, seventy sons (Judges 8:30). But even with all those wives, Gideon also had a son, Abimelech, who was born to him by a concubine.

Now, in a political culture where hereditary rule is the custom, there's a problem when the ruler has seventy sons. The competition, I mean to say, is complicated. That's when Abimelech, an unlikely candidate as the son of a concubine, asserted himself. He went to the area, Shechem, from which his mother had come, and threw out a challenge to leading persons among his kin: "'Which is better for you, that all seventy of the sons of Jerubbaal rule over you, or that one rule over you?' Remember also that I am your bone and your flesh" (Judges 9:2).

The leading men of Shechem found this a convincing argument. They gave Abimelech seventy pieces of silver, with which he hired "worthless and reckless fellows" and killed all seventy of his half-brothers "on one stone." All, that is, but Jotham, the youngest son in the large family. This is where the trees come into our story. One would think that Jotham, just glad to be alive after his siblings had been wiped out in multiples, would have slipped out of the country as quickly and quietly as possible. Instead, Jotham stood on the top of Mount Gerizim and made a speech, directing it specifically to the leading men of Shechem who had assisted his half-brother in the murderous enterprise. He told them how the trees "once went out to anoint a king over themselves" (Judges 9:8). They went first to an olive tree. If you've been to the Middle East, you know that this was an admirable choice. Olive trees have the tough, gnarled look of survivors, and you learn that many of them are several hundred years old; guides in Israel will tell you that some of the olive trees you see may have been there when Jesus walked by with his disciples. The roots of the olive tree manage to pry their way through the rocky soil down to a place where they can survive the long dry season and where the soil can store the nourishment of the early and latter rain.

Today, the olive tree is prized for its cooking oil. In ancient times, it was equally sought for its healing quality. Thus, as Jotham unfolded his little parable about the trees and their search for a leader, he portrayed the olive tree as brushing aside the invitation to serve as king of the trees: "Shall I stop producing my rich oil / by which gods and mortals are honored, / and go to sway over the trees?" (Judges 9:9).

The presidential search committee had to feel a bit rejected; their first choice had been quite dismissive in his reply. But they were not discouraged. They simply lowered their expectations a notch and approached the fig tree. Mind you, the fig tree couldn't compare with the hardy olive tree. Some figs, in fact, grow on bushes. But the fruit is delicious, and humans have been eating it since prehistoric times. Long before anyone knew that figs were rich in sugar, calcium, and iron and that they could be especially tasty if a baker made them into fig-filled cookies, people knew that they simply tasted delicious. And the tree in Jotham's parable knew as much too. So the fig tree answered, "Shall I stop producing my sweetness / and my delicious fruit, / and go to sway over the trees?" (9:11)

The committee had been rebuffed twice, but there was still a grand prospect, the grape vine. Mind you, a vine doesn't really give you the feeling of a tree. It's not what comes to mind when you hear Joyce Kilmer's words, "I think that I shall never see / a poem lovely as a tree." But as the ancient saying goes, beggars can't be choosers, so the search committee went to call on a vine. Probably it was difficult to be quite as buoyant in their presentation as when they approached the olive and fig trees, but I sense that the trees gave the matter their best pitch. The vine's reply was rather like the fig tree's: "Shall I stop producing my wine / that cheers gods and mortals, / and go to sway over the trees?" (9:13).

By now I think you've noticed a decisive similarity in the responses of the three candidates. Not only have they refused the offer, they've done so in a rather condescending way, all with the same phrase: should they leave their important work "and go to sway over the trees." Clearly, the olive tree, the fig tree, and the grape vine didn't have a high opinion of kingship. To produce olives, figs, or grapes was an enviable assignment, but being a chief executive was— well, it was pretty perfunctory: just to "sway" prettily from time to time.

It makes one feel that either Jotham had a poor opinion of governance, or that perhaps he had somehow read a twenty-first century newspaper or had watched the late evening news on television. It's really quite astonishing how much time governors, presidents, and queens spend in making people feel good, not simply entertaining heads of state, but also greeting teams that have won the World

Series or the Super Bowl or persons who have recently made a headline that gives them temporary news value.

But this shouldn't surprise us, because when these people were running for office, we heard only occasionally about their platform—indeed, even the platform itself, the summation of the candidate's thinking, came to us in sound-bytes that appealed more for being memorable than for conveying an idea. Sometimes we confessed as much by saying, "I don't really know what it is, but I just *like* so-and-so." So it is that we get someone to "sway" over us.

And mind you, I haven't even touched on the way prospective votes are courted on the basis of support from some athlete or entertainer, or the attention that is paid to the appearance or demeanor of the candidate's spouse.

Maybe Jotham had a point when in his parable of the trees he made it appear that we see the major function of a king or a president or a governor as to "sway."

I'll come back to all of that in a moment, but let me return to this tree-election. After Jotham suggested that productive trees didn't care for this ceremonial job, he made his most sarcastic point. The delegation of trees then went to the *bramble* and said, "You come and reign over us." The bramble produces no fruit and has no obvious value. But even the bramble has pride—and even the bramble has aspirations.

> And the bramble said to the trees,
> "If in good faith you are anointing me king over you,
> then come and take refuge in my shade;
> but if not, let fire come out of the bramble
> and devour the cedars of Lebanon." (Judges 9:15)

If you're wondering what happened following Jotham's venture into political discourse via his parable of the trees, I can tell you that he knew his life was in danger. Rising politicians don't like to be characterized as bramble. And, of course, the more insecure the person, the more unnerved they are by ridicule. So Jotham fled, in fear for his life. And

Abimelech, the murderer of his seventy half-brothers, had a brief and disastrous reign. He led an attack on the city of Thebez, and when it appeared that he would win, "a certain woman threw an upper millstone on Abimelech's head, and crushed his skull." Fearing that people would say a woman had killed him, Abimelech appealed to his young armor-bearer to draw a sword and kill him. And the biblical writer concludes the story, "and God also made all the wickedness of the people of Shechem fall back on their heads, and on them came the curse of Jotham son of Jerubbaal" (Judges 9:53-57).

So that's the story of the day the trees held an election. Jotham, the storyteller—whom I would also classify as a political philosopher, the kind of person whose opinions one would find nowadays in the op-ed section of a newspaper—obviously didn't think much of kings. And it's equally clear that he didn't think much of the wisdom of the voters: in this case, the people who had elevated their relative to a position of political power.

I have to tell you that this parable frightens me. We humans are all political creatures, whether we choose to be or not, because to live in a world with other persons means to bring ourselves under some system of laws and civic structure. The people of ancient Shechem raised up a king—"elected" him, in their own fashion—and those of us who live in democracies raise up all sorts of officials, from school board members to presidents of nations.

It is a good system. Sir Winston Churchill put it this way in a speech to the House of Commons in 1947: "Democracy is the worst form of Government except all those other forms that have been tried from time to time." I proudly identify myself as a voter, and because I have been blessed with a long life, I have voted in seventeen presidential elections.

But I'm worried, and that tree election tells you why. Too many of the most qualified people have an attitude too much like the outlook of the olive, the fig, and the grape.

They see their present occupation as more significant to the welfare of the planet than the role of persons in government. *Politician* has become a dirty word. More than two hundred years ago, the great Samuel Johnson said, "Politics are now nothing more than means of rising in the world." In saying so, Johnson could have gotten his text from Jotham: the bramble was willing to become a king.

While waiting for a plane on a September day in 1961, I ventured a conversation with a handsome, young African man who, like me, was flying to Nairobi, Kenya. Since there were no reserved seats on the plane, we sat together and continued our conversation on the flight. In becoming acquainted we exchanged passports for a moment. I noticed immediately that his occupation was listed as "politician." I said cautiously, "That word has an unfortunate connotation in America." He was not offended. Instead he responded with pride, reminding me that the root word meant citizen, and that he saw himself as a man who was dedicating his life to the service of people. Indeed, he saw "politician" as being his calling under God, as real as my calling to be a minister of the gospel.

My newfound friend was returning to Kenya to work with Mr. Kenyatta in establishing a new government in that land. Just the day before, Mr. Kenyatta had made his first public address since being released from political prison. Josiah Kariuki was young, handsome, intelligent, and articulate. And he was proud to give his life to be a politician.

As it turned out, he did just that. Perhaps two years later, I purchased the book Josiah had written, and I knew he was well on the way to the career to which he had dedicated himself. But a few years after that, as I was reading the *New York Times,* I came upon a tiny international news item. A young political leader in Kenya, Josiah Kariuki, had been assassinated by his political enemies. Josiah's idealism, his political genius, his dedication to his people, had been wiped out.

It is famously said that a nation gets the leaders it deserves. I think that's what Jotham was trying to say when he told how the trees held their election. After all the centuries of human history, after kings and presidents and prime ministers and dictators, we still haven't adequately learned our lesson.

CHAPTER 7

AS FAIR AS THE RAIN

Scripture Reading: Matthew 5:43-48

If you love nature, and more particularly if you love literature about nature, you're probably familiar with the name of Aldo Leopold. In his little classic, *Sand County Almanac,* Leopold tells about some of his experiences on the rural property he had purchased. One day, he had to take down a great oak tree that had been killed by lightning. The tree was thirty inches in diameter and had lived through many years and several owners.

Leopold needed only a dozen pulls of the saw to cut through the few years of his ownership, years in which he had learned to love and cherish the farm. Then the saw began to cut through the years of the farm's previous owner, a bootlegger who had hated the farm. The man had skinned the farm, Leopold said, of its "residual fertility, burned its delinquent taxes, and had disappeared among the landless anonymities of the Great Depression."

But Leopold noted that "the oak had laid down good wood" for this previous owner; the sawdust was as fragrant, as sound, and as pink as for those more recent years when Leopold had lovingly tended the farm. The nature writer concluded, "An oak is no respecter of persons."[1]

That's what Jesus said to his disciples one day. He chose a different figure of speech from a different act of nature, but testified to the same remarkable generosity in nature.

Jesus was using this quality in nature to persuade his listeners that they ought to treat one another kindly, and that they should do so without any prejudice. Even if the other person was not good or was unappealing or was even manifestly unkind, still the rule was the same. "Love your enemies." And just in case we want to keep that love on a quite theoretical basis, Jesus spelled it out: "and pray for those who persecute you" (Matthew 5:44).

I don't have to tell you that Jesus was calling for a standard of conduct that doesn't come easily or naturally. As far as I can see—and I suspect your response is somewhat akin to mine—my instinct when meeting human conduct as Jesus described it is likely, at best, simply to avoid that person, or at worst, to find some way to get revenge. Or to put it more delicately, to see that folks get their just due. We believe in playing fair. If someone is nice to us, we're nice to them in return. In truth, that's quite logical. On what ground, then, does Jesus appeal to us to treat everyone graciously and even to pray for those who do us wrong?

Quite simply, so that we will be children of God. We want to be children of God, don't we? If so, we need to know what God is like. Jesus proceeded therefore to give a standard for measure and recognition. Look, Jesus said: God makes the sun to rise on the evil and on the good, and God sends rain on the just and on the unjust (Matthew 5:45). And that's the way we should relate to people too.

Well, some of us will confess that this is what bothers us about the rain and the sunshine. They're so *impartial*. They bestow their favors without discrimination, on good and evil persons, on deserving and undeserving, on rich and poor, on every ethnic and national group. The sun and the rain aren't impressed by our social standing or our bank account. Still worse, they aren't impressed even by our morality or our true worth. As Aldo Leopold reported, the oak laid down good wood and fragrant sawdust as gladly for the abusive bootlegger as for the ardent naturalist. You may curse the sun and complain against the rain, but they will continue to bless you with their inestimable wealth.

That's the way God is, Jesus said. God is the one in back of the sun and the rain, and God sends them forth generously and without partiality, on the evil and the good, the just and the unjust. We find it hard to understand this quality in God, just as we do in nature. But then we come to the uncomfortable, unnerving part: Jesus said that we should be the same. We should relate to people with just such careless, quite illogical generosity. If we do, we'll begin to act like God.

I'm quite sure that Jesus' audience was distressed by what he said. "Love your enemies," Jesus said—and he said it to an audience who was intimately acquainted with enemies and with hatred. William Barclay says that the Jews of the first-century world were involved in a double hatred—the world hated them and they hated the world.[2] The Roman historian Tacitus said that the Jewish nation was the "vilest of people"[3]; but the Jews, by no means to be outdone, said that Gentiles were created by God to be fuel for the fires of hell.[4]

Jesus was speaking to people who knew truly violent hatred, as both subject and object, so when he insisted that we should love everybody, including even our enemies, the people had a dramatic context for hearing what he said. Jesus was speaking to people who had suffered oppression for generations, some of it so brutal as to build up reservoirs of revenge. And to such a people as this, Jesus said that we should be like our Heavenly Father, who sends rain on the Gentile as gladly and as freely as on the Jew, who is equally generous to the deserving and the undeserving.

Well, if that kind of preaching made Jesus' first-century audience uncomfortable, I'm sure it has very much the same effect on us. It does, at least, if we listen thoughtfully. We may be too civilized to be so direct and outspoken about our feelings, but it's clear enough that our generation doesn't look any more kindly on its enemies than have other generations. Ours is a society where there is still a tenuous border between races and classes and ethnic groups, so that bitterness slips out at unexpected times and also in unlikely places. It's a world where people still paint swastikas on synagogues and where some of the worst hatred sometimes shows itself on college campuses, a place where intellectual civility is supposed to reign. People of different political and social convictions sometimes see each other with a refined—and sometimes an unrefined—feeling of contempt.

So we need, as much as people did in Jesus' day, to listen when our Lord speaks of the goodness of the rain. He didn't say, "Don't hate your enemies." His statement was positive and far more demanding: *Love your enemies. Do good to them. Bless them. Pray for them.* Then Jesus provided a standard of measurement, because qualitative language really needs some quantitative reality: be like the sun and the rain. They are utterly impartial.

What did Jesus mean when he commanded such all-inclusive, non-discriminatory love? I suspect that you and I are likely to feel hopeless when we read Jesus' words, reasoning that such love is simply out of our reach, so there's no use even trying. Let me try, therefore, to explain what Jesus was saying, so we can grapple with his command.

We will understand Jesus better if we examine the word for love that is used in Jesus' commandment. The English language, especially as popularly used, has only one word for love, so we use the same word whether we're speaking of our family, our country, the weather, a movie, or a restaurant. Greek, the language in which our New Testament was written, had four words for love, so it was possible to speak much more precisely and thus to make a point more crisply and clearly. I won't go into all four words except to say that one had to do especially with family love, another with passionate love, and still another with brotherly love. None of these words is used in this passage in which Jesus commands us to love our enemies. Rather, it is the remarkable word *agape*.

This word means *unconquerable benevolence; invincible goodwill.* The late William Barclay explained that when we regard a person with *agape,* it means that no matter what that person does to us, no matter how she or he may insult or injure us, we will never allow any bitterness against them to enter our hearts. Instead, we will regard them with that unconquerable benevolence that seeks nothing but the person's highest good.[5]

On that basis, let me make several distinctions. For one, I don't think we are commanded to love our enemies the same way we love our families. This would be neither good sense nor good religion. The Greek language, as I suggested before, was a very precise language, and the New Testament partakes of that exactness, which is surely to our advantage in understanding. If we were supposed to love everyone with the love of family, it is logical that the Greek word *stergein* would have been used, rather than *agape.*

And of course, we must clear our minds of the idea that love is a warm, fuzzy feeling, a cuddly coziness. Love is much more than warm feelings, lovely as such feelings are to all of us who are fortunate to experience them in one form or another. Love is also (and especially) action and conduct. We know as much from the experiences of our daily lives. A mother loves in those moments of warm emotion when she embraces a child, or snuggles a baby after its bath. But she loves the child also in the routine of diapering, packing lunches, and cleaning up household messes. In truth, we would be suspicious of her love if it showed itself only as warm feelings.

When it's a matter of loving our enemies, or loving all humanity (which can be a very motley lot, if we are realistic enough to consider the collection honestly), I don't know that warm feelings have a great deal to do with it. Someone has said that in the matter of loving our enemies, love is not so much something of the heart as it is of the *will.* When we speak of those who are dearest to us, we sometimes use the phrase, "falling in love," as if to show that we can't help what has happened to us. Loving our enemies, however, is usually a quite different matter. We have to use our will and our discipline to do it. Someone has defined *agape* love as the power to love those whom we do not like and who do not like us. I don't think this is a fully satisfactory definition, because for a Christian, *agape* love ought to include the lovable and the unlovable. In that connection, perhaps we could note that such love works with those we love even when they're not that appealing—that is, when they do something that is irritating or thoughtless or rude. But the large point, it seems to me, is that *agape* love simply rises above feelings, whether good or ill.

Keith Miller helps our understanding in his book, *A Second Touch.* He says that after he became a Christian, he felt he ought to have a warm, selfless feeling toward everyone. He gradually discovered that Christian love is not necessarily such feelings, but the act of service in Christ's name. He reminds us that the greatest act of love was Christ's death at Calvary. But before Jesus went to Calvary, he prayed in Gethsemane to get the strength to fulfill the assignment. The love that took him to Calvary was not a special kind of feeling; rather, Jesus had to put concentrated will into the act. Miller goes on to say that our greatest days of loving may be those in which we don't even feel well, much less loving.[6]

So the love we seek, if we want to love as God loves, is not really a matter of emotion—which is usually what we associate with the concept of love—but a quality of character. But perhaps you've discovered that if we exercise this will to love, a warm and fulfilling emotion frequently follows. I like that feeling, and I think it can rightly be said that such a feeling demonstrates that God has created us humans in such a fashion that we are at our best when we do what is right, so of course we feel happier when we respond to life with love. But the good feeling is not the issue. We should love, not because it makes us feel good, but because we have a new character—a character that can truly be described as *godly*: we are like our Heavenly Father, who sends rain on the just and on the unjust.

Let's look again at the sun and the rain, as they reflect the character of God. How is it that they can bestow their benefits regardless of the quality of the recipients? For one thing, because they're bigger than their circumstances. I am sometimes unloving in my conduct because I don't have the stability of character to withstand the circumstances I encounter. The other person's irritability quotient is stronger than my patience quotient! The sun and the rain aren't like that. It is so much their nature to perform their functions that the conduct or the attitude or the distastefulness or the degree of worthiness in the recipient cannot sway them from their course. Their created disposition is stronger than the negative factors in their human receivers.

Now, of course, you and I aren't programmed for conduct as the sun and the rain are. It is up to us to choose how we will respond, which means that we have to contend with all sorts of difficult emotions if we are to respond lovingly to certain individuals and their conduct.

It may seem ironic, but this kind of response is sometimes more difficult for moral—"good"—people than for those whose conduct is not so good. That is, just as a person who has no sense of pitch is not troubled when someone sings off-key, so someone who has no sense of ethics is not likely to be troubled by dishonest conduct. In truth, I think some people consciously seek to toughen their moral judgment, so to speak, in order to cope with the world in which we live. Thus, we hear comments such as, "Look, that's just the way it is in the world of business, and you might as well get used to it." Or again, "Well, politics is like that. You shouldn't expect anything better."

But persons who strive to be moral and honorable *are* troubled. They have tuned their moral ear to a pitch of honesty, and dishonest conduct rasps on the hearing of their soul. I'm sure that many in Jesus' first-century audience were like that—not only the Pharisees, who were often scrupulously honest, but Jesus' own hardworking fishermen, who offered a good product and expected to be treated well in return.

So see this in the nature of God: God doesn't wink the divine eye at evil, and God doesn't suggest that our conduct doesn't matter. Quite the contrary. But God doesn't allow the conduct of others to determine the divine character. The divine character isn't controlled by the moods or personalities with which it deals. Nor should we allow our characters to be so controlled.

Why not? Why be generous in our attitude toward all?

I think there are two answers, and both are quite pragmatic. For one, we will never overcome evil by responding with evil. To the contrary, if we become unloving, then evil has won. There is always the possibility that when we treat an undeserving person kindly, that person may change in time. There is always the possibility that somehow, some time, goodness will break through.

And second, good is worth doing whether it "works" or not. Right is right, whether or not it is acknowledged, and love is love, and purity is pure. We respond with a certain type of character because we have chosen, by grace, to belong to a certain family—the family of God. Jesus said that God is like this, as impartial as the rain—and you and I ought to demonstrate the same family trait.

NOTES

1. Aldo Leopold, *Sand County Almanac* (New York: Oxford University Press, 1966), 9.

2. William Barclay, *The Mind of Saint Paul* (New York: Harper, 1958), 9.

3. Tacitus, *Histories,* 5:8.

4. Barclay, 10.

5. William Barclay, *The Gospel of Matthew,* vol. 1 (Philadelphia: Westminster Press, 1958), 172.

6. Keith Miller, *A Second Touch* (Waco, Tex.: Word Books, 1967), 88.

CHAPTER 8

LIVING IN HIGH PLACES

Scripture Reading: Habakkuk 3:7-19; Psalm 18:31-33

W hen we hear the word *deer,* most of us picture what may be the most graceful of all four-legged creatures, an animal that runs and bounds with such ease and elegance that it seems as if its creator had set it to music. Personally, when I think of a deer, I have a sentimental picture, because my daughter—now in middle age—cherished the deer as her favorite of all animals from preschool until I really don't know when. "Flag the Fawn" was her imaginary friend for a very long time. Some, of course, see the deer as their favorite hunting prey, and others as a peril of the highway at particular seasons of the year.

An encyclopedia will tell you, rather matter-of-factly, that deer "are the only animals with bones called *antlers* on their heads" (I confess that I didn't know that this is their singular distinction), and that there are more than sixty kinds of deer (which includes moose), and that some live in the heat of the desert while others live in the lands above the Arctic Circle, and that they have ranged in size from one foot high and weighing twenty pounds, to seven-and-a-half feet high and more than 1,800 pounds.[1]

But several great souls a very long time ago—souls especially sensitive and spiritual, persons we identify as prophets and poets—saw the deer as a creature that dared to live dangerously, in high places. I see them therefore as symbols of saints, of persons who choose to live close to God.

One such dramatic reference is attributed to David, the King of Israel and the poet beloved to millions for the psalms that bear his name. The book of Second Samuel reports on the perilous days when young David was being pursued by the then King of Israel, Saul—a man to whom David was intensely loyal but who nevertheless realized that David was his primary contender for the throne, even though David himself had no such ambitions at the time. After one occasion when David escaped Saul's pursuit, he "spoke to the LORD" his gratitude for deliverance "from the hand of all his enemies, and from the hand of Saul" (2 Samuel 22:1). The same grand song appears also in the Book of Psalms. In the midst of David's eloquent hymn of thanksgiving, he speaks of God's care this way: "He made my feet like the feet of deer, / and set me secure on the heights" (2 Samuel 22:34; Psalm 18:33).

This is an interesting phrase in the midst of a warrior's song. At other places in this song, David recalls a time of absolute peril: "The cords of death encompassed me; / the torrents of perdition assailed me; / the cords of Sheol entangled me; / the snares of death confronted me" (Psalm 18:4-5). In such a time, he "called upon the LORD; / to my God I cried for help" (18:6), and in time "He brought me out into a broad place; / he delivered me, because he delighted in me" (18:19). Some of David's language is as robust as an Olympic champion's or a conquering general's: "By you I can crush a troop, / and by my God I can leap over a wall" (18:29). But it's the picture of the deer that stands out to me: David feels that God has blessed him with feet that allow him to be "secure on the heights."

And then there was a man named Habakkuk. Where David was a warrior king and a poet, Habakkuk was a prophet of God. Like many of the prophets—perhaps most of them—Habakkuk lived in hard times. Times so difficult, in fact, that his faith was pressed to the very limits. He begins his record this way:

> O Lord, how long shall I cry for help,
>   and you will not listen?
> Or cry to you "Violence!"
>   and you will not save? (Habakkuk 1:2)

Habakkuk lived in a time when evil seemed to reign on all sides, when people disregarded whatever was right, and it seemed that nobody cared. But worst of all was this: with cruelty, crime, and injustice at every turn, it seemed that even God was unconcerned, almost as if God were shrugging divine shoulders at evil.

So the prophet cried to God for help. Why call to God when God seems detached and indifferent? I suspect because there's nowhere else to turn—and also because something in our human psyche insists that God *must* care. Some inextinguishable insistence in our souls continues to call on God no matter how useless the call may seem.

And God answered. But the answer was such that Habakkuk may have wished he hadn't pressed the matter. "Yes," God said, "I see that there is evil and violence in the land, and I'm going to do something about it. I'm going to send judgment on your nation, by way of the Chaldeans."

You've heard of physicians warning that the remedy is worse than the sickness. The prophet must have had such a feeling. He objected that the Chaldeans were worse than his own people. How could they be used as an instrument of justice or of reproof?

And God replied, "If [the answer] seems to tarry, wait for it; / it will surely come, it will not delay. / . . . but the righteous live by their faith" (Habakkuk 2:3-4)

So Habakkuk said that he would wait. No matter how great the wickedness of the wicked, or how inscrutable the judgment of God, he would wait. He was sure, absolutely sure, that in the end, justice and right would be done.

But as the prophet makes his declaration of faith, I wonder if there rose in his mind a vision of the kind of disaster that might befall him. Perhaps something in a dark corner of his consciousness said, suppose it *all* goes wrong? Suppose what you're now experiencing is only the beginning of trouble? What then? Will you still believe? Some person might have put such questions to him; such dubious friends lurk in the path of every soul. I'm inclined, however, to think that Habakkuk put the questions to himself. And he answered:

> Though the fig tree does not blossom,
>   and no fruit is on the vines;
> though the produce of the olive fails,
>   and the fields yield no food;
> though the flock is cut off from the fold,
>   and there is no herd in the stalls,
> yet I will rejoice in the LORD;
>   I will exult in the God of my salvation. (3:17-18)

I love this man, Habakkuk. I would want him on my side if life were tumbling in all around me. He's the one I'd call if I'd just lost my job or if my family had turned against me or if the doctor had just given me an altogether dismal report.

Can you imagine a more unreserved and dramatic declaration of faith? Even if all of nature, God's sovereign domain, should turn against Habakkuk, the fields and flocks go barren until starvation is camped at his door—even then, he says, I will "rejoice in the LORD." And if you think that perhaps "rejoice in the LORD" is a generous translation, let me tell you that it is really a rather weak one. The Hebrew words, the scholars tell us, should be phrased literally, "I will jump for joy in the Lord."

Now here's the question that comes to you and me: whatever in the world could make a person talk like that? I ask this, not as a psychological study (indeed, it would be unseemly to play with the emotions of a person as deeply moved as Habakkuk is in this writing). I want us to know what drives Habakkuk because there are times in all our lives when our world seems to collapse around us. One thinks of persons caught in a flood or a tornado who lose not only their home and their money but also some of their most cherished, sentimental possessions. Is there any chance for us, in life's shattering moments, to feel the confidence the ancient prophet felt? And especially given Habakkuk's feeling that perhaps even God wasn't on his side or, at the least, was indifferent to his predicament. Habakkuk tells us his secret. He is confident, so confident that he casts his faith in sublime poetry:

> GOD, the Lord, is my strength;
> he makes my feet like the feet of a deer,
> and makes me tread upon the heights. (3:19)

When life is hazardous in the extreme, when the future is without measurable certainty, and when even the justice of God seems remote and unsure, a person needs surefootedness of soul. Then one can walk on the precipice of disaster, down even into the valley of the shadow of death. One can leap, even, over the crevasses of illness and despair. The sheer mountainside of defeat can be scaled. God makes my feet, this man says, like the feet of a deer, so I can tread upon the heights!

Habakkuk, like David, had watched the deer often. You and I are probably inclined to picture the deer as a graceful, calendar-picture creature that lives in the forest or grass country, or if we're fortunate, we see as it grazes along some roadway. But the deer of ancient Palestine found its home more often in the craggy hillsides of that rocky land. David and Habakkuk had watched a deer leap almost casually from one ledge to another, over crevasses and along narrow paths, until it would stand at last on some sheer pinnacle. If the lion was king of the beasts, this deer was king of the heights. So Habakkuk would say, as he took inventory of his soul, "God has made me like that! I can live on the heights. No passage of life is too challenging for me." What a magnificent way to live! What a sense of fullness in life! These writers—people of grand faith—took for their symbol and purpose not an animal that would destroy or one that would live in docile ordinariness, but one that could survive with grandeur in high places. The psalmist and the prophet both saw themselves, under God, as people called to lives of challenge.

Mind you, we can go through life without such heroism. The safest way to do so is to stay on low ground. There's no place to fall if you locate yourself in a marsh. The peril comes when you venture to higher ground.

The principle is quite simple. If we aim for nothing, we'll never miss. But when we set a demanding goal, one that by most measures seems out of reach, or when we take a position of character, or declare a purpose in life—well, then, in doing so, we are open to personal disappointment and public embarrassment. If we're content to be no better than we are, we won't suffer the pain of disappointment in this world—or at least not until we're quite old and have come to the age of possible remorse. The stretch and strain of life and the possibilities of defeat come with the striving, with the hunger for more of God, and more of Christian character, and more of the basic challenge of living.

People sometimes get the impression that if they become Christians their troubles will be over. I suspect that a certain kind of preaching has encouraged such thinking, but I must tell you that this isn't so. Now mind you, I am altogether sure that by becoming believers, we will be better equipped—dramatically so!—to deal with whatever troubles and tests may come. But becoming a Christian doesn't make us exempt from trouble. We live in a world where problems exist, and becoming a Christian doesn't mean moving out of the world; it means facing its issues with courage and purpose. At its best, it means living in high places!

And here's why. When we take the Christian faith seriously, we find ourselves open to new struggles, struggles we'd never know if we remained thorough-going secularists or timid religionists. There's no danger of falling when you're a cynic or a full naturalist, because there's no place to fall; you're already there. The peril comes when we believe largely and grandly. There's little danger of being disappointed if you're always expecting the worst. You won't be let down if you never take a chance on people, or if you trust only those who are sure winners. The apostle Paul said, near the end of his journey, "for I know the one in whom I have put my trust, and I am sure that he is able" (2 Timothy 1:12). That's dangerous! So dangerous for Paul, in fact, that he ended life as a martyr. Some people tell me how little they believe and expect me to praise their intellectual acumen. I want, rather, to say, "Coward! Why not test faith a bit, out where your feet can't touch the ground?"

Habakkuk would have faced no issue if he had adjusted himself to life's injustices or if he hadn't ventured his faith. He could have looked at the evil in his world, shrugged his shoulders, and said, "That's just the way life is." If he had, he would have suffered no emotional or spiritual strain and no struggle of the soul. Instead, he envisioned justice and morality, and he argued with life when it seemed less than just or moral—and as he did, he was forced to walk on life's "high places," where you need the feet of a deer if you're to survive.

Earnest believers sometimes look pathetic, even absurd. They declare such high ideals and such grand dreams and then can't always fulfill them. Those who are critical accuse them of being hypocrites, and the cynical say they're naïve. But sometimes what the person on the street thinks is naïve is actually the vision of a better world and a better life. And what is sometimes easily disposed of as hypocrisy is nothing less than raw courage: the courage to set a goal somewhere beyond one's sure grasp. The poor, earnest fool who sets such a goal for himself or herself may fall face-forward while trying to reach it. But hear me: while falling, such a person gets farther than the critic who stands secure on life's low ground.

I cast my vote with Habakkuk and David. David, the warrior-king, is the stuff of legends. He dared to challenge Goliath when older warriors trembled in their armor. He held to his integrity when it would have been easy to take advantage of King Saul's erratic ways. He believed in God with such assurance that he was compelled to sing it out, because God "made my feet like the feet of a deer, / and set me secure on the heights" (Ps 18:33).

The paths of our lives often run through rugged and uneven ground. In truth, one doesn't have to search for places of peril; in one fashion or another, we encounter such places in the so-called normal course of events. And those of us who cast our lives with God are not exempt from these common perils. To the contrary, a godly life often compels us into still more hazardous places.

So is there an advantage in becoming a person of faith, a follower of Christ? There is, indeed—and I am speaking of our lives on this planet, without even entering the long-term promise of eternal life. I am convinced by my study of Scripture, by the lives of great souls whom I have known firsthand and in stories, and by my own experience, that the Christian faith opens new reservoirs of strength, and that life in Christ opens up vast new possibilities of fulfillment.

That's the kind of experience and confidence that the long-ago prophet Habakkuk knew. He took up the same figure of speech that David the poet had exercised several centuries earlier:

> I love you, O LORD, my strength...
> He made my feet like the feet of a deer,
>   and made me secure on the heights. (Psalm 18:1, 33)

The call of a godly life is a call to stand, to walk, to run on *high places*. Don't fear it; rejoice in its potential. God can give us feet like the feet of a deer, so that we will walk in high and wondrous places, and know that we will emerge victorious.

NOTE

1. *The World Book Encyclopedia,* vol. 5 (Chicago: World Book, 1987), 74.

CHAPTER 9

AN ANT IN THE PULPIT

Scripture Reading: Proverbs 6:6-11

Students in my homiletics classes will tell you that I am quite fierce in my commitment to good preaching. I still like the old-fashioned synonym for the pulpit, the "sacred desk." Though I have preached thousands of sermons, I have never gotten over the awe of being accorded with the responsibility and privilege of being trusted with people's minds, hearts, and souls for those minutes that constitute a sermon.

So just what do I mean when I speak of "an ant in the pulpit"?

Well, for one thing, I'm thinking of the wise Benjamin Franklin, who through his favorite pseudonym, "Poor Richard," said well over two hundred years ago, "None preaches better than the ant, and she says nothing." Even with my regard for Franklin and his many clever sayings, I might disregard what he said, perhaps out of respect for my lifelong calling. But I suspect Franklin got his idea from an ancient and sacred source, the Old Testament book of Proverbs. Listen:

> Go to the ant, you lazybones;
>   consider its ways, and be wise.
> Without having any chief
>   or officer or ruler,
> it prepares its food in summer,

and gathers its sustenance in harvest.
How long will you lie there, O lazybones?
When will you rise from your sleep? (Proverbs 6:6-9)

As I indicated earlier in this book, the Bible chooses often to make a point by directing our attention to lessons from nature. Solomon's legendary wisdom, as I've said, was exhibited by the extent of his knowledge of the birds and beasts and even the insects of our world—wonderful creatures that know how to cope successfully with the peculiar challenges of their specific environments.

And of those creatures that are familiar to most of us, no one does it better than the ant. The author of Proverbs says as much by choosing the ant for one of the most difficult of sinners, the lazybones. There's no one harder to convert than the person who is in love with his erring ways, since one isn't likely to change his or her ways until those ways come to seem abhorrent. So the wise man chose the ant to give this sermon to the comfortable sinner. That's why I dare to bring the ant into my imaginary pulpit.

For many a city dweller, an ant is simply a pest to be avoided and, if necessary, eliminated. We're not naturally inclined to see the miracle that is an ant. Consider, for instance, the ant's longevity compared to other insects. So many insects come and go within a day or a week, but a worker ant can live as long as seven years, and a queen ant, fifteen. Some scientists think that it is this longevity that has helped the ant develop its remarkable abilities. So it is that ants develop miniature "farms." They collect and store seeds, they milk tiny "cows." If they must cross a dangerous road, they have been known to dig a tunnel under the road. They make pets of certain other insects, they use tools, and—unfortunately—they even make war and capture slaves. One wonders who taught the ant such mechanical and social skills—or perhaps I should say, certain antisocial skills.

I wonder if little boys—and girls, too, for that matter—

still watch ants, or if the remarkable world of the ants has been pushed aside by mechanical and electronic marvels that, by comparison to ants, are really quite ordinary. I remember the ants that would suddenly appear at a crack in the sidewalk, finding the only exit in the concrete jungle humans had made. And I remember marveling as an ant carried some crumb of bread several times its size and weight, tugging it quite rapidly to its storage place. At such moments, it seems to me, some adult always appeared to admonish, "That's the way you have to prepare for the winter, boy." It was the era of the Great Depression, but it was also the era when people believed in economizing, regardless of what the stock market said, and when any farmer or homemaker or laborer was enough of a philosopher to find wisdom in the simplicities of life.

And that's the sermon the ancient wise man found in the ant. He didn't talk about the social and organizational abilities of the ant, though I'm quite sure he or some of his friends knew about such, because those long-ago generations knew so much about nature simply by living intimately with its wonders. But Solomon, the wise man, was fascinated and impressed by the ant's sense of industry and its desire to prepare for the future. By a host of ingenious methods, the ants prepare for each winter. And they do this, the writer of Proverbs said, without having any chief, officer, or ruler. Perhaps the Bible simply meant that the ants are without the legal disciplines that control our human lives. But as far as science now knows, the ant literally has no "chief or officer or ruler." A colony of ants, they tell us, can be as small as ten ants or as populous as the city of San Francisco, and each ant will have its specific responsibility, yet no ant rules the colony.

I wonder if each ant knows instinctively its place in the system? Or is it perhaps in the nature of the ant to cooperate for the common good? Whatever it is, each ant seems to fill his or her place in the work of the colony. And they do so with remarkable ability. One man watched an ant that had come upon three pieces of food. Each piece was about twice the size of the previous one. The ant went to three other ants and touched antennae with them. The three then scurried to their nests and came back with helpers. There were twenty-eight ants to handle the smallest piece of food, forty-four for the next piece, and eighty-nine for the largest piece—in almost perfect proportion to the size of the burden. And they all went to work.

In many parts of the world, labor is honored with a holiday. In Puerto Rico, the United States, and Canada it is celebrated on the first Monday in September, and in Europe, on May 1. Australia has such a day but calls it "Eight Hour Day," commemorating the struggle to limit the length of the working day. These celebrations are seen as civil holidays, but I would make a case for thinking of Labor Day as a religious holiday, too, because I believe in the sacredness of labor.

I say this because the Bible story begins with God at work, creating the universe. The day of rest was a celebration of the work that had been done in the six days preceding. I think those generations that see the honor of work are better able to see the sacredness of the day of rest. Carl Sandburg imagined God as a worker:

God gets up in the morning
    and says, "Another day!"
God goes to work every day
    at regular hours.
God is no gentleman for God
    puts on overalls and gets
    dirty running the universe we know
    about and several other universes
Nobody knows about but Him.[1]

I like Sandburg's playfully reverent picture, because I'm so sure that God has privileged us humans by providing us with something productive to do. Jesse Stuart, the Kentucky writer who endeared himself to a generation with his novels and essays, suffered a severe heart attack while making a speech at Murray State University and spent the better part of a year regaining his life. When he could again pick up a pencil to jot down a thought or the beginning of a poem, he felt his manhood beginning to return. One day, a young man appeared at his door and introduced himself as "Young Joe Smith." Stuart saw that he was a square-shouldered man of about thirty, with large hands that were soft now, and that he was wearing boots, though they were inconsistent with the rest of his garb. "These boots make me feel a lot better," he explained.

Stuart then got Young Joe's story. He had worked with a tree company (thirty-three cents an hour, in a world quite different from our day), and he was an expert at what he did. But one day, a giant limb crashed down from a tree, breaking four of his teeth, fracturing his skull in nine places, and bursting his right eardrum, leaving him deaf in that ear.

But what was worse, from Joe's point of view, was that the accident destroyed his balance, and equilibrium is crucial to a tree climber. "So when I was in the hospital, I asked for my climbing boots," Joe continued. "After wearing boots eleven years, I got lonesome for them. My doctor had my wife bring them to the hospital. A lot of people laugh when I tell them about this. They don't understand why I wanted my boots."

Jesse Stuart answered, "I can see why you did." And Stuart recalled what it did for him, as he hovered for days on the edge of death, to see his latest book and some magazines carrying his stories. Lying on a table next to his hospital bed, these articles gave him the heart to fight his way back to work.[2] I think it was this sense of the holy gift of work that made the British poet John Oxenham pray that if God would see that his work was done, he wanted not to linger on, a "workless worker in a world of work."

There is, indeed, sacredness about work that leads to a worthy pride in work well done. I remember Charlie, who worked at the desk in front of me on the swing shift in a factory office. We kept some of the accounts for the factory supplies, in old-fashioned hand posting. Charlie's books, with their perfectly shaped numbers and never a smudge, were beautiful to behold. There were others in that office whose daily motivation seemed nothing more than the lunch break and the closing whistle, and who lived each week primarily for the paycheck on Friday night. But Charlie was proud of his neat, almost artistic, bookkeeping. I observed this contrasting scene week after week. I was working the swing shift so I could go to college during the day. Along the way, I encountered Edwin Markham's poem of social protest, "The Man with the Hoe," a battle cry against those forces that made such a laborer "dead to rapture and despair, / A thing that grieves not and that never hopes." My youthful idealism resented a system that did such to "the Thing the Lord God made and gave / To have dominion over sea and land."

And I am troubled still for talents that never have opportunity to find their potential because social structures, or neighborhood influences, or tired and perhaps insensitive teachers or counselors don't see the hidden gift or hear the mumbled dream. When I see a parent or grandparent praising the kindergartener's crayon gift of the day, I ponder the children who bring home equally attractive work—perhaps, in fact, much more skilled and imaginative—but with no one who has the time or the energy to appreciate the art. How many artists, architects, or poets are lost before the third grade because their talent is disposed of before it has time to shape into a dream?

I think that the issues of human labor have become still more complicated in our time. It is not only that some never have a fair chance to discover their talent; others discover theirs but are afraid to follow its call. When my son asked a successful attorney if he enjoyed his work and got a very tentative answer, he followed up, cautiously, with a second question: Was there something he'd rather be doing, another career he wished he had followed? Without hesitation, the man answered, "I wish I had been a middle school gym teacher." He had followed someone else's dream for him rather than his own.

I wonder how many people are doing work they don't really enjoy because another work—one they really like—is not held in as much regard; or even more likely, because it doesn't pay as well. And I wonder, further, about the way we reward labor. I wonder why we pay so much to those who take care of money compared to what we pay those who take care of our minds. Or to put it more directly, how do we explain the disparity between the salaries for those who are in all sorts of executive positions and those who teach us to add and subtract, or to parse a verb, or to understand the principles of democracy or finance?

We have a friend who has skills which are, to me, quite astonishing. He runs a small business that he describes as "Your Neighborhood Handy Man." He can fix anything in a house. By contrast, I do well to turn on the right light switch. He tells me that he admires my ability to address an audience and to put my ideas into a book. I have equal regard for his ability to repair all the things I don't understand, and I gladly pay him accordingly. He takes great pride in his work, and with good reason.

I wonder what it is that gives some people pride in what they do, while others seem only to work for a piece of money and are apparently content with a slipshod effort and product. I see the difference every day, at every level of life. One flight attendant makes me feel that it is, as the recorded announcement declares, a pleasure to serve me, while another makes me feel that he or she can hardly wait to be done with all of us passengers. I choose some service lines at the bank because some tellers bless my day with their enthusiasm or their graciousness. Some preachers prepare their sermons with the kind of loving care that convinces me that they believe they are working for eternity. As it happens, I believe they are too. But as it also happens, I believe that the checkout clerk, the taxi driver, and the professional athlete are also working for eternity. That is, I think that God—the Ultimate Worker—judges us humans on what we do with the sacred trust of our time and our talent.

Do I sound impossibly idealistic? If so, I must answer that I speak with some experience. I grew up in a working class home, in a working class neighborhood, and along the way, I have worked at a variety of jobs, for some of which I was not especially qualified. The best I can say for some of my efforts is that I sincerely tried, though I hardly distinguished myself. In the course of my rather long life, I have been privileged to know a vast variety of people at work: physicians, teachers, public officials, corporate executives, farmers, truck drivers, professional athletes, scientists, computer specialists, salespeople, servers, and clerks. Really, the list could be almost without limit. I have learned that satisfaction in one's work is not a result of the level of remuneration, though for some, abundant remuneration dulls the pain; nor is it public recognition, though there is always something momentarily intoxicating when people pay you deference because of your role. But the satisfaction in work comes in doing it well, and in believing that it is worth doing.

In other words, the kind of satisfaction that is native to the ant. Apparently, the ant is just made that way, committed to doing its task and happy to fulfill its particular role. But you and I aren't ants. We are susceptible to temptation, so that we may shirk a bit if no one is looking, and we may, at times, be content to give a project something less than our best effort. And perhaps still worse, we may take a job that we sense isn't really right for us because we're impressed with the title or we think others will be impressed, or because of what the work pays—forgetting that no slave master is more cruel than money.

I have no desire to be an ant, but I'm ready to hear the ant's sermon—especially because the ant preaches it, as Benjamin Franklin said, without saying a word. But what the ant does instinctively, you and I have to do by choice and intention and sometimes by firm resolve. We may learn from the ant, but we do our work by the character of someone made in the image of God—the ultimate authority on work.

NOTES

1. Carl Sandburg, "God Is No Gentleman," *Honey and Salt* (New York: Harcourt Brace and Jovanovich, 1963), 29.

2. Jesse Stuart, *The Year of My Rebirth* (New York: McGraw-Hill Book Company, 1956), 234-36.

CHAPTER 10

A BUSH THAT BURNS
AND BURNS

Scripture Reading: Exodus 3:1-6

Something happened to Moses one day that he never forgot. It changed all the rest of his life. To be still more emphatic, I dare to say that what happened to Moses changed the course of human history.

By the time of this life-changing experience, Moses had spent roughly 14,600 days tending sheep in the land of Midian. If you are inclined to mathematics, you've already calculated that 14,600 days is just a way of spelling out forty years, a way of making you realize just how long forty years can be. Because, as we live life forward, we don't live it by the year but by days—and sometimes by hours or minutes within the days. Life can get very "daily."

But after you're past the initial shock of 14,600 days, you may want to remind me that Moses didn't really tend sheep all of those days. After all, there were weekends, so we can subtract over 4,000 days from that number. And even if Moses had to work a six-day week, the way our grandparents did, we can still subtract over 2,000 days from that forty-year total.

Sorry. They didn't have weekends in Midian, and they didn't have a six-day week. Especially where shepherds were concerned. Sheep are not the wisest of animals, and those who want to take advantage of them—like wolves and thieves—don't take off weekends. Thus, the people who tended sheep had to tend them all the time. One wonders why anyone would ever want to be a shepherd. I think some people probably liked it—for example, people who loved solitude or who found great pleasure simply being outdoors. But I suspect that most of the people in that ancient world who were shepherds didn't know there was any other way of life. Nobody visited their areas with job fairs or offered vocational tests to find out a boy's or a girl's best skills. Most shepherds probably came from a long line of shepherds, generations and generations of shepherds, who were wonderfully at home in the rumbling wilderness.

But not Moses. He hadn't planned to be a shepherd and may never have known a shepherd at firsthand until he became one. He had been trained to be a ruler or perhaps a counselor to rulers, or perhaps simply to be a comfortable gentleman, living a life of privilege. In the mercy and providence of God, he had been raised in pharaoh's court, enjoying all the benefits of a superb education in Egypt, where learning was held in esteem. And I suspect he expected to enjoy such privileges himself.

One day, however, Moses saw one of the people of his blood, an Israelite, being humiliated by a slave driver. Somewhere in Moses' soul, there was a passion for justice. He responded to the injustice in a rush of righteous anger. He attacked the slave driver and killed him. I don't know if this was his intention or whether he simply let his righteous indignation get out of control, but none of that mattered very much. Moses was now, suddenly, a fugitive from justice. That's how he ended up as a wilderness shepherd. So whatever his youthful dreams may have been, by the time our story begins, he had accumulated more than 14,000 routine days, time enough to think there was nothing more to life than routine.

And that's when Moses had the experience that changed his life so dramatically that today we know him as the first great emancipator and as one of the world's greatest law-givers, a figure of such dominance that he now ranks among the legendary figures of human history. Moses saw a bush, and that made all the difference. Now, let it be said early that bushes aren't naturally the stuff legends are made of. It's not that I have anything against green, growing things. In truth, the one request I have for my study window is that it should look out upon trees. But, of course, it's easy to make a case for a tree—like a giant sequoia for an obvious example. One can imagine someone having a life-changing experience in the presence of a tree that simply overpowers by its age, its unassailable strength, and its commanding beauty. But a *bush?* I remember a poem we learned in the ninth grade that encouraged us to be a tree if possible, but if not, to be a bush—and if you couldn't be even a bush, be a "scrub in the valley below." But, of course, the scrub itself is a kind of bush. Bushes just don't reach out and grab you. No matter what the poet said, bushes don't insist that you can be more than you are or more than you've previously thought of being. Bushes aren't like that.

In fact, there's a sense in which bushes have no particular standing of their own. The encyclopedia describes a bush as "any woody plant that is smaller than a tree and does not climb." It has many branches, "but no main central stem." The description goes on to distinguish between a bush and a shrub, and mentions that the tumbleweed is, in a sense, neither.[1] I remember when I was traveling through Africa many years ago I was told at a certain point that I was in bush country. As I looked over those vast stretches of land, I got the impression that "bush country" was not a designation of praise.

But it's good to remember that life can have its epochal moments almost anywhere. No matter whether it is flowers or people or sunsets or bushes, you never want to sell short the influence that may be felt in someone's life and in ensuing human history. As Moses tended his father-in-law's flocks, he led them "beyond the wilderness," until he came to "Horeb, the mountain of God" (Exodus 3:1). There's an ominous sound in that phrase, "beyond the wilderness." If I were a movie director, I think I would introduce some rather quiet but dissonant music as Moses walked into shadows and we sense that he is moving into the unknown, the mysterious, and the numinous. And here, suddenly, there is "a flame of fire out of a bush."

The biblical writer tells us that Moses looked. I should think so! Then: "I must turn aside and look at this great sight, and see why the bush is not burned up" (3:3). I am impressed by Moses' response. I think I might simply have hid my eyes while beating a cautious retreat. But this may indicate why Moses became a great emancipator while I've been content with a simpler life. If Moses had fled the scene, we wouldn't be reading his story several thousand years later.

God spoke to Moses from the bush, calling him to lead his people, the slave people Israel, out of their bondage and into a heritage God was preparing for them. Moses talked back to God. I think he was a very pragmatic sort. That's why he had the courage to examine the bush that burned and was not consumed. So when God announced a special, quite harrowing assignment, Moses began giving reasons why he wasn't qualified for the assignment. Eventually, God won the argument, but it wasn't for Moses' failing to hold his ground.

And what follows, of course, constitutes my argument that this event was one of the watershed events of human history. Moses became the great emancipator—in a sense, the model for every such charismatic leader since then. His exploits in leading a band of former slaves through a wilderness for some forty years and bringing them to the edge of the land of their promise is the stuff that legends are made of. And it all began when Moses' attention was captured by a bush in the wilderness of Mount Horeb.

As you might imagine, scholars have examined this

story in their usual cautious, sometimes imaginative, some-times skeptical way. Some think the bush was of a species that, at a certain time in its development, gets a fiery color. Others suggest that Moses' impression came because of the peculiar way the sun struck the bush at that particular moment. Still others argue that Moses may have suffered some minor heat stroke, causing him to have an illusion. I have trouble with all these explanations on the basis of cause and effect: that is, when you have an extraordinary effect, the cause must be sufficient to explain such an effect. When I see a man who is rational enough that he looks at a phenomenon of nature, not with superstitious fear but with what can perhaps be called scientific curiosity, and who, when he encounters something quite beyond explanation, chooses still to argue its issues in the fashion of a quite pragmatic mind—and then, allows himself to be led into a venture so full of setbacks, frustrations, and losses that even a very dedicated person would give up—but instead this man remains steadfast to the end: well, well—you need quite a cause to get such an effect.

Mind you, what happened that day at the bush was only the beginning of the story. Moses was reinvigorated again and again to deal with the problems he encountered. There was more to his experience than just the bush. But it all *began* with the bush, and I find this very impressive.

So at this point, I'd like to ponder the principle of the bush that burns and keeps on burning. Because as I see it, the grand miracle of that strange day is not that the bush continued to burn for moments or perhaps hours after Moses first saw it but that its effect kept burning in his soul for the rest of his life. And I raise this point because—just because!—you and I may have our bushes too.

I'm thinking, as some of you might have guessed, of what Elizabeth Barrett Browning said. "Earth's crammed with heaven, / And every common bush afire with God."[2] I suspect that some would disregard Miss Browning's words as sentimental enthusiasm, but her life supported her words. When she was fifteen, she injured her spine in a fall so that she tended to invalidism. Her brother's death caused her to isolate herself still more, until she came to spend most of her time in a darkened room. But in her isolation, she wrote poetry and letters, and some of her poetry caught the fancy of another young poet, Robert Browning.

Their story has become one of the most famous romances of all time. Elizabeth was 38 when they met, and Robert was 32. They married privately because her father opposed their romance so vigorously, but before long, they eloped to Italy. Eventually, they had a son, when Elizabeth was 43. She died at 55, a far cry from the young woman who had shut herself off in semi-invalidism for years. Not only did she and Robert make their mark as poets, and not only did their home become a favorite spot for notable English and American artists and writers; more than that, she became a vigorous social advocate, especially in attacking the practice of child labor and in her opposition to the injustices suffered by countries that were controlled by other nations.

Miss Browning found the image for her poem in Moses' experience, and she extended Moses' experience to include any who would have the faith and daring to see it. She believed that "every common bush" was afire with God's presence. Perhaps some would feel that by applying Moses' experience so broadly, she was minimizing it. I don't see it that way. I think she was reminding all of us that God is waiting to speak to any of us who might be willing to be shaken out of our ordinariness. After all, it had happened to her. True, she was a talented woman, enough so that her father published a book of her poetry when she was still a girl of thirteen. But she was also a woman who was retreating further and further into a world of seclusion, of willing invalidism. Almost surely, Robert Browning's romantic attention helped set her free. But he couldn't have done it alone; Elizabeth had to cooperate. She could have allowed herself to remain shut up in her illness and her melancholy for her brother. Somehow, somewhere, Elizabeth saw a common bush that burned—and its burning lit up all the rest of her life.

Does every human being sometime, somewhere see a bush that burns? Alfred Lord Tennyson, England's most popular poet in the latter half of the nineteenth century, challenged himself and all of us by way of a flower: not a flower that wins a prize at the county fair, but a flower any of us might see. Tennyson found it in a "crannied wall," plucked it out, "root and all," then held it in his hand, just a "little flower." But he wondered, as he held it there, "*if* I could understand / What you are, root and all, and all in all, / I should know what God and man is."[3]

I'm sure Tennyson was being intentional when he described his flower as being "in a crannied wall"—that is, in a place where, more likely than not, it would be overlooked. Indeed, perhaps it was stumbling upon the flower in just such a place that set his mind pondering that the very mystery of God and man was like this, embodied in a plant of no particular distinction and in a place where it would be pushed aside or crushed by any passing foot, or perhaps in such a sheltered place that only a careful traveler would find it.

Which brings me back to Moses, and to you and me. Moses was forty years—over 14,000 days as I said earlier—in the wilderness, tending sheep, before he saw the bush that grasped him for history. Were there other bushes, earlier, that he could have seen if he had been open and ready to do so? Or on the other hand, might Moses instead have missed the bush that day he noticed it? What if he had been so preoccupied, so caught up with the economics of shepherding, or with the concerns of family, or perhaps with the irritations of working with his father-in-law—what if, then, he had seen the bush but not stopped, not cared?

In my rather long lifetime of listening to the stories of God's presence in our world, sometimes from notable souls whose witness has moved thousands, but more often from the rather routine people in the churches I've served or in churches where I've preached for a weekend, I have marveled at the way God is at work in human life. I have marveled, too, at the many vehicles by which God's voice is spoken to us humans, sometimes in the events of the day and often in some encounter with nature. When I sum up these stories, I realize that most of them are like flowers in a crannied wall, like a "common bush" that, in a particular moment in someone's life, becomes an agent of the Holy Spirit.

I believe, with Gerard Manley Hopkins, that "the world is charged with the grandeur of God." But I'm painfully certain that you and I can miss this grandeur, or that we can reduce it to ordinariness, so that it doesn't shock us into meeting God in a deeper way. Eugene Peterson is right when he warns about the danger of "habitual indifference to the glory of a dogwood in blossom."

Human history has only one Moses, and whatever the nature of his encounter that day with a bush on Mount Horeb, there is a sense in which there was only one such bush. But there is only one you, too, and something in me is very sure that there is a bush somewhere in your life and in mine. You may come upon it by chance, perhaps in an airplane conversation with a stranger you'll never see again. It may be hidden in a crannied wall, or part of the vast, apparent sameness of bush country.

And it may very well be a common thing. In fact, the odds lean in that direction. On a common day, tending to your common tasks—sheep or whatever—you come upon still another bush: a person, a neighborhood walk you make each morning, the subway you always ride, the commute you travel by your own automatic pilot. But suddenly, the common comes aflame, and you begin fumbling with your shoes because you sense this is holy ground.

"Earth's crammed with heaven." Crammed! Even today. *Especially* today.

NOTES

1. *The World Book Encyclopedia,* vol. 2 (Chicago: World Book, 1986), 607.

2. Elizabeth Barrett Browning, *Aurora Leigh,* bk. 7, l.821.

3. Alfred Lord Tennyson, "Flower in the Crannied Wall," 1869 (italics his).

CHAPTER 11

THE UNIVERSE WITHIN

Scripture Reading: Psalm 8:1-9; Psalm 139:13-17

When we begin to contemplate the wonders of God in nature, most of us travel too far too soon. For those adventuresome enough and willing to invest enough, Antarctica has become the destination of choice. The travel brochures tell us that this least-inhabited continent is breathtaking in its beauty. I believe them. But as one who spent several scores of years driving on winter's icy roads in the upper Midwest, I'm not especially anxious to gaze out on millions of acres of ice.

Mind you, I don't mean to minimize any of the wonders of nature. After all, when Job insisted that he wanted a chance to make his case with God, the Lord God took him on an extended tour of creation. Seeing nature under the right circumstances is a premier way of looking into both the wonder and the heart of God. In Job's case, God sometimes seemed simply to be having fun with him: "Where were you when I laid the foundation of the earth?" (Job 38:4). Then again, God took Job to a kind of celestial art gallery: "Have you entered the storehouses of the snow?" (38:22). We're told that no two snowflakes are alike; we could study them a lifetime and still be amazed.

But you don't have to be Job or take his journey to marvel at our creation. Even the dullest soul catches his breath on a star-flung night or when watching the sun rise some spectacular morning. And animals! Not one of us hasn't experienced or heard stories about the loyalty of a family dog, or the almost neurotic character of a thoroughbred horse, or the sense of superiority in the family cat. My few travels in the Middle East made me nod in vigorous agreement when an Archbishop of Canterbury said that his most vivid impression of Egypt and Israel was the condescending look on the face of the camel. Believe me, the wonders of nature are everywhere, from the spider to the leviathan.

But there are wonders to be seen without going to Antarctica, Africa, India, or the islands of the sea. A glass-bottomed boat is wonderful, and a diving suit is probably even better. But if you're looking for a cheap trip that will take your breath away, just look in the mirror. You're it. Even on your poorest days, you're it. There's nothing in creation more wonderful than you.

The psalmist made the point roughly three thousand years ago. He started his nature trip the way all of us might, looking at the stars. And, of course, he was getting a better view of the stars than you and I can hope to gain. It's a rare night when our urban or suburban skies are clear enough of the clutter of artificial light that we can see the heavens in their ecstatic wonder. "When I look at your heavens," the psalmist said, "the work of your fingers, / the moon and the stars that you have established; / what are human beings that you are mindful of them, / mortals that you care for them?" (Psalm 8:3-4).

I know the feeling, and I suspect that you do too. Even to the unaided eye, the heavens are so vast, so overwhelming, and so utterly magnificent that we humans seem insignificant. But suddenly, the psalmist interrupts himself, as if he has been arrested in his thoughts. "Yet you have made them [humans] a little lower than God, / and crowned them with glory and honor" (Psalm 8:5). Wonderful as is the world of space—and who would deny or seek to minimize that wonder?—the poet realizes that we humans are ourselves quite remarkable. The Creator has chosen to make us only "a little lower" than himself, and has chosen further to crown us (as if we were royalty!) "with glory and honor."

The psalmist examined the wonder of himself on another occasion; this time not in the context of the wonders of the heavens, but in his enchantment with the quality of the very God. He marveled at God's attention to us humans ("Even before a word is on my tongue, / O LORD, you know it completely"), and the divine omnipresence—wherever he goes, God is there. And from that marveling, he ponders the wonder and mystery of his own person: "I praise you, for I am fearfully and wonderfully made" (Psalm 139:4, 14). He recognizes God's creative genius in his own human makeup, announcing to God his happy conclusion: I'm quite a piece of work, and You did it! As Robert Alter's translation puts it, "I acclaim You, for awesomely I am set apart."[1]

So what is it about us humans that is so remarkable? To begin with, we could talk about our beginnings. Ursula Goodenough, one of America's leading cell biologists, puts it this way: "I start with my egg cell, one of 400,000 in my mother's ovaries. It meets with one of the hundreds of millions of sperm cells produced each day by my father. Astonishing that I happen at all, truly astonishing."[2] Astonishing, indeed! I'm surprised that I'm even here. And as I read Professor Goodenough's statistics, I ask myself what person I would be if it had been a different egg cell out of that vast number, or a different sperm cell. I would have the same parents, but how different would I be?

Then, after getting past the miracle that we are even here, we can start examining our basic equipment, most of which goes generally unnoticed unless something seems out of order. Each of us began with a single cell, but in the miracle which is invested in each of us each day, our bodies wear out and replace about two billion such cells. We have more than six hundred muscles—most of which, obviously, we are never conscious of—and if the skin of a medium-sized adult were spread out, it would cover some twenty square feet, though it weighs only roughly a pound. The outer layer of that skin is replaced entirely every fifteen to thirty days, because our bodies have a quite unbelievable renewal system. God not only made us well, but so equipped us that as certain parts wear out, the system constantly provides their successors.

Our bodies need a supply of fuel to provide energy for our continuing operation. We have a relatively simple system for taking in the fuel—food, we call it—but a quite intricate system for changing that fuel into energy, via our digestive system, and then for distributing the energy through the body, to all of its diverse parts. The small and large intestines, which constitute the major part of the digestive system, are some twenty-seven feet in length. When one considers the varieties of food we put into our bodies, and sometimes the irregular fashion in which we do so, we can only marvel that the system handles this fuel with only occasional complaints.

The blood serves as the delivery agent, bringing food and oxygen and carrying away carbon dioxide and other wastes. The blood is sent on its tasks by that strange and wonderful engine we call our heart. It begins its work when the human fetus is only three weeks old, and it beats a hundred thousand times a day—summer, winter, holidays, happy days, grumpy days; cared for or not, appreciated or maligned, it keeps beating. By the time we're seventy years old, the heart has pumped no less than 46 million gallons of blood through the body.

And then of course there is that still more mysterious instrument, the brain, which is the control center of the body. The eye says that it's just a grayish-pink, jellylike ball marked by a number of ridges and grooves. At birth, it weighs less than a pound, and it reaches its full weight of about three pounds by the time we're six years old. But it receives and copes with all the information we need, both from within and without the body. It stores up information and retrieves it for us on call—though sometimes we fumble in the retrieval process and wonder what's wrong with our brain. And it asserts its rights. Although it makes up only about two percent of our body weight, the brain uses some twenty percent of the oxygen when the body is at rest. If it is deprived of that oxygen for three to five minutes, the damage to the brain—and thus, to the whole person—can be serious and perhaps irreversible.

It is with that little three-pound mass that Shakespeare wrote his sonnets and plays, Johann Sebastian Bach his chorales, and Dorothy Sayers her mystery stories. With the brain, the neurologist learns all that we know about the brain, and with it, the inventor develops its ally, the computer. With it, too, we must confess, someone writes pornography, and someone else plots a murder, and still another person develops a financial scheme that will defraud a substantial number of his or her fellow citizens. In some people the brain is a restless creature, constantly in search of ideas and adventure, while in others it seems content to dwell in the effortless lowlands of life, never stretching itself, never seeming to ponder its own potential.

We are remarkable creatures, we human beings. Walt Whitman, the wide-ranging nineteenth-century poet wrote, "And the narrowest hinge in my hand puts to scorn all machinery," and he was right. The contemporary essayist, Brian Doyle, marvels at "[t]he dart and dance of your tongue! The throb of your heart, the flash of your mind, the fact that your knees and elbows work!"[3] And he is right to marvel so. And Shakespeare writes, "Lord, what fools these mortals be!"[4] And he, too, is right. No wonder the psalmist said that we are fearfully and wonderfully made.

But, of course, I've touched on only the surface of the matter, the skimmed surface of what you and I are. Eugene H. Peterson, pastor and scholar and Bible translator, speaks briefly about the wonder of our physical bodies, and then continues, "And that of course is just the physical. There is far more that cannot be weighed: thoughts and knowledge, feelings and moods, dreams and visions, words and numbers, prayers and songs, faith and love and hope, habits and memories. Most, in fact, of who and what we are cannot be discovered by cutting us open and examining our guts."[5]

Albert Einstein put it this way. "The most beautiful emotion we can experience is the mystical. It is the source of all true art and science. He to whom this emotion is a stranger, who can no longer wonder and stand rapt in awe, is as good as dead." Something in us reaches out beyond ourselves. We reach out to other people, to animals, and to inanimate nature; we reach inward to nooks and crannies of our own souls that startle us by their strangeness. We ask questions: Why am I here? Suppose I had been born to other parents: who, then, would I be, and would the person I now am never have come into existence if I had not been born when and where I was? And what is this world all about, and what is my purpose in this world? Would it make any difference if I had not been born?

These are questions that, as far as we know, only human beings ask. So it is that anthropologists, regardless of their own measure of religious faith, describe us humans as *Homo religious*. That is, we humans are uniquely religious. We reach out to God. We're sure Someone must be out there. As the apostle Paul said, "Ever since the creation of the world [God's] eternal power and divine nature, invisible though they are, have been understood and seen through the things he has made." Unfortunately, as Paul goes on to explain, we humans haven't always gone on to know God, and we "did not honor him as God or give thanks to him"; instead, we became "futile" in our thinking. "Claiming to be wise, they became fools; and they exchanged the glory of the immortal God for images resembling a mortal human being or birds or four-footed animals or reptiles" (Romans 1:20-23).

But however poorly we may pursue our religious instincts, or however poorly even the most devout may live out faith's precepts, we humans reach out for God. And of all the wonderful things that can be said about us, this is the greatest of all. I am in awe of our human ability to build the Cathedral of Notre Dame or a naked skyscraper, or to compose a poem or a symphony. I marvel each time I see an infant begin to shape words: how is it that we know how to contract our throat, elevate our tongue, and purse our lips to make a sound like the adults around us, whether that tongue be English, Korean, French, or Urdu? I marvel, too, that we laugh and cry, despair and aspire. You are right, brother psalmist, we are fearfully and wonderfully made, from our toes to the tops of our heads. But above all, I am in awe that something in us wants God—and that something in us is profoundly satisfied when we sense the reality and the nearness of God.

This is what interrupted the psalmist's soliloquy to the stars so long ago. Looking at their vastness, he wondered how we human beings could possibly matter—only to realize that you and I are even more awesome than the stars because God has chosen to make us only a little lower than the divine.

This is, of course, a quite audacious statement. A tough-minded, cynical soul might tell the psalmist to "come off it"; we're not really that great. But we *are*. We are loving, hating, aspiring, debasing, creating, copying, wise, foolish, generous, miserly, beautiful, ugly, loveable, despicable creatures. And it is this very contrariness, this capacity for the extremes that shows how remarkable we are. If we were unfailingly good and noble and beautiful and productive, we would be automatons. Instead, we are creatures with apparently infinite capacity who also possess the power of choice, and with that power, we shape not only our own lives, we also impact the lives of other humans and of institutions and of the planet on which we live. Which is wonderful, yes—and also, fearful.

So what do we do about ourselves? We should start by acknowledging the wonder of what we are, and thank God for the investment that has been made in us. Scientists estimate that there are currently thirty million species on our planet, of which we humans are only one. But such a one! So begin with the wonder of that fact, marvel at it, and thank God for it.

But, of course, the only way to thank God properly is to use with sensitive care the gift God has bestowed on us. The rest of creation seems to do its thing without thought or resistance. I suppose we can't really say that a tree or the grass or the planets or the fish are trying to cooperate with God. They are simply being what they are. But you and I, we remarkable creatures: we decide whether we will co-operate with God. Indeed, God invites us to converse with him through the medium of prayer, and having received such a royal invitation, we respond to it quite casually and matter-of-factly, many of us accepting the invitation only when we see it as especially necessary or valuable. And as for the larger responsibility and opportunity of cooperating with God, I suspect that it doesn't too often occur to the average human mind. Some people think about it a great deal and live accordingly. We call those people saints. It's the way all of us should seek to live.

The ultimate, way-out fact about us humans is an-nounced early in the biblical story, when the writer of Gen-esis tells us that we are made in the image of God (Genesis 1:26-27). The story goes on to report that we have proceeded to mess things up very badly, but the fact remains that we're made of good stuff, from a unique and exquisite pattern.

That's why, when we're inquisitive about the wonders of creation, you and I should look in the mirror. Then look deeper, farther than any glass can reveal, and see how God has invested the divine image in us. And at that moment, pray that we may seek daily to fulfill our God-ordained potential.

NOTES

1. *The Book of Psalms: A Translation with Commentary* (New York: W. W. Norton, 2007), 481.

2. Ursula Goodenough, *The Sacred Depths of Nature* (New York: Oxford University Press, 1998), 60.

3. Brian Doyle, *Daily Guideposts, 2009* (New York: Guideposts, 2009), 167.

4. William Shakespeare, *A Midsummer Night's Dream,* act 3, sc. 2, l.115.

5. Eugene H. Peterson, *Tell It Slant* (Grand Rapids: William B. Eerdmans, 2008), 133.

CHAPTER 12

EDEN EVERY MORNING

Scripture Reading: Psalm 104:10-24

Great Britain has blessed the world of children with a number of poets and storytellers. One thinks immediately of E. E. Milne and *Winnie the Pooh,* Beatrix Potter and *Peter Rabbit,* Robert Louis Stevenson and *The Children's Garden of Verses,* and the rollicking poetry of Edward Lear and Hilaire Belloc, to name a representative few. But perhaps no one was more loved by children in the British Isles or published more books than Eleanor Farjeon. She once said that she was "singing songs before she could write and even before she could speak, and as soon as she could guide a pencil she began to write them down." When she died in 1965 at age eighty-four, she had published more than eighty books of stories and poems for children.[1]

No doubt she wrote "Morning Has Broken" for children, since they were so surely her preferred audience, but it is as engaging a piece of theology as one is likely to find. I'm sure I'm prejudiced about Sundays, so I agree readily with John Newton when he describes Sunday as "day of all the week the best," and the quality of the day has a head start for me if the worship service includes Farjeon's poem/hymn.

Farjeon subtitled her poem, "For the First Day of Spring." I suspect that the inspiration came to her on such a day, and I agree that it is a perfect way to enter that lovely season. But the wonder of the poem, of course, is that on such a day the poet found herself transported into the days of creation. "Morning has broken," she sang, "like the first morning; / blackbird has spoken / like the first bird." And the wonder of it all is that she is experiencing this as it first came, "fresh from the Word"—for the biblical book of Genesis tells us that God created by *speaking* each unfolding act, and the New Testament writer identifies Christ as the Word by which the world came into existence (John 1).

So it is that I recommend Farjeon's poem not only for the first day of spring, but as the right way to begin every day. What better than to look out on a new day—*any* new day—as an unspoiled gift from the hand of God, "fresh from the Word"?

Another British poet, Gerard Manley Hopkins, would understand what I'm trying to say. A Jesuit priest with devoutness even beyond his profession, he exulted, "The world is charged with the grandeur of God." So charged, in fact, that even though it now "wears man's smudge and shares man's smell," it nevertheless keeps its pristine quality: "nature is never spent; / There lives the dearest freshness deep down things."[2] It is this "dearest freshness deep down things" that can be counted on to give us a new Eden any morning.

Eden. The very word conveys a kind of magic to the soul. The word comes from a Hebrew word meaning "fertility," signifying the "abundant vegetation" that characterized the garden.[3] But as the book of Genesis describes it, Eden was more than a place of exquisite natural beauty and even of lush abundance. It was also a place of divine trust; humankind was "to till it and keep it" (Genesis 2:15). This apparently unlimited store of sustenance, beauty, and wonder was being left in humanity's care, the wealth of the ages in what proved to be fallible, erratic hands.

And there was more. It appears that this Eden was so pleasing to God that the Creator enjoyed "walking in the garden." That is, there was something about the garden that was more than material sustenance and more even than aesthetic nourishment for the soul. It was a place of divine pleasure. I submit that when we humans relate rightly to nature, we enter into this divine pleasure. We know that nature is not God and is therefore not to be worshiped, but that God has invested so much in nature that when we are willing, we can touch God through the grandeur he has invested in nature.

Ursula Goodenough, a professor of biology with particular prominence in the study of cellular biology, identifies herself as "a non-theist." But she looks upon nature with a sense of gratitude that makes her write:

> Imagine that you and some other humans are in a spaceship, roaming around in the universe, looking for a home. You land on a planet that proves to be ideal in every way. It has deep forests and fleshy fruits and surging oceans and gentle rains and cavorting creatures and dappled sunlight and rich soil. Everything is perfect for human habitation, and everything is astonishingly beautiful.
>
> This is how the religious naturalist thinks of our human advent on Earth. We arrived but a moment ago, and found it to be perfect for us in every way.[4]

Perfect, indeed. Specialists, whether studying beetles or the planetary movements, find wonder in the complexity of the objects of their study and the peculiar precision with which they operate. Poets, who are sometimes described as the guardians of language, stretch almost to exhaustion to find words to describe what they see, so that Gerard Manley Hopkins invents a few words, and E. E. Cummings settles for "which is natural which is infinite which is yes." And the hobby gardener straightens up from hours of puttering and pottering and says, "Beautiful!"

Perfect? Yes, more perfect than any of us—specialist, poet, or untrained observer—can ever fully comprehend.

So how do we respond rightly to such a wonder as this? The wise writers of the book of Proverbs urged that we *learn* from nature—even the ant, the badger, and the spider. Jesus, too, told us to learn from nature, and he pointed to the lilies of the field and to the generosity of the sun and the rain. The Hebrew prophets found spiritual tutors in the world of nature. One of them, Isaiah, told his audience that the ox was smarter than they were, and another, Habakkuk, wished as he sought for high places in faith that he had spiritual surefootedness to compare with the agility and grace of the mountain deer. We can learn from nature, no doubt of that. If we approach nature with even a modicum of humility, she will teach us.

But these days, we are realizing increasingly that it isn't enough to get philosophical or poetic insights from nature; we need to return to our ancient assignment described in Genesis: we are supposed to take care of our planet. We are the stewards of nature. A good planet is hard to find, and since we've been blessed with such an extraordinary one, we had better do right by it. If we don't, we shouldn't be surprised if it talks back to us—indeed, kicks back at us, explosively and perhaps devastatingly.

We humans—especially and almost uniquely in the western world—are so taken with the idea of *progress* that we have rarely asked the price when we've been told what we "must do" in the name of progress. And let it be said that we have done some wonderful things, and those wonderful things should not be disparaged as we examine the promises of progress. I rejoice when I'm eating a handful of grapes because progress found a way to eliminate the seeds without my having to spit them out. I remember a morning nearly fifty years ago when the manager of the dining room in a hotel in Lagos, Nigeria, proudly showed me a homegrown banana; it was a third the size of any banana I would have found on an American breakfast table, but for this Nigerian, it symbolized progress just as the one in our stores back home did.

But we're coming increasingly to realize some of the price we're paying for "progress," and of course, we can't begin to know what price our grandchildren and their descendants will pay. Gerard Manley Hopkins sensed it more than a century ago, as the cities of his native England came more and more to be shaped by the Industrial Revolution. So he saw a world where "all is seared with trade; bleared, smeared with toil." Perhaps even Hopkins would be without words to describe how trade has now seared our landscape by turning nature into millions of acres of concrete parking lots to service our seemingly insatiable desire for still one more shopping mall.

"Green" is currently becoming the "in" word. More and more people in more and more areas of public concern are urging us to watch our consumption of fuel and our treatment of nature lest we find that this perfect planet become uninhabitable at the worst, and stripped of its native charm at the least. This is an area where everyone with a Christian conscience should let their voices be heard—but far more important, they should make their conduct exemplary. We are not making a better world by buying more things, but by taking the time to enjoy what we already have; and most particularly, by investing more of ourselves in people and in our own character development. *Things* have become the distraction that keeps us from experiencing life and love and people and God.

I realize that the green movement will not give us Eden, because Eden is more than grass and trees and animals and birds and clean water; Eden is a place where God is nearer and where our human relations are elevated by this consciousness of God's presence. But changing our treatment of nature's resources will unclutter our lives to a degree where there is a better chance of hearing God's voice. Sinclair Lewis, the twentieth-century American novelist who often seemed to be at his best when mocking sincere but inept people, tells of an evening when George Babbitt and his friend Paul Sinclair were on vacation at Lake Sunasquam. Babbitt awkwardly asked his friend how the lake struck him. Paul answered, "Oh, it's darn good, Georgie. There's something sort of eternal about it." And the author comments, "For once, Babbitt understood him."[5]

The lake is not eternal, but the feeling is. And while Babbitt and his friend were not eloquent—no poets, they!—they felt the eternity of that moment as deeply as Gerard Manley Hopkins might have. We all have that touch of Eden in our souls. But my point is, we can have it more often—and I venture God would be pleased if we did.

I mentioned earlier that Eleanor Farjeon dedicated her writing almost exclusively to children, but that the poem that has become a hymn is packed full of theology. One wonders if Farjeon expected children to get it? Personally, I'm confident she did. She wasn't one to talk down to her readers, nor was she one to underestimate their capacities. I suspect she knew that what children lack in intellectual training they make up for in innate perceptiveness—and perhaps especially in their refusing to let literalism get in the way of reality.

We adults lose our appetite for Eden. After so many battles with the real world, as we experience it, we find it hard to imagine that things can be perfect. So it is that a child can sing, "Sweet the rain's new fall / sunlit from heaven," while adults calculate what the rain will do for market futures or for the prospects of this afternoon's ball game. I remember a summer morning nearly half a century ago. As I returned from a walk, I picked up an earthworm from the sidewalk and took it to my then four-year-old daughter, who couldn't have a dog because the parsonage was next door to the church. "I've got a pet, I've got a pet!" she squealed. I wouldn't trade ten seconds of childish ecstasy for a full day of adult disillusionment. Eleanor Farjeon was quite right to tell children that the first day of spring is a return to Eden and this blackbird that sings is "like the first bird." And she was more than right in thinking that children would get it.

My appeal is for us to claim Eden every morning. Will it last for the full day? I doubt it. In many cases, we'll be glad if an Eden on any particular day lasts for an hour. But for that hour, we see our Lord passing, and we walk with him in the garden of our faith. Without a doubt, we'll have to get more childlike if we're to experience this Eden. We'll have to drop some of the adult cynicism we've nurtured for so long. And we'll have to take down some of the walls we've built to protect ourselves from disappointment. The disappointment is simply a reminder that the original Eden has been lost, but it isn't proof that we can't regain it for a few moments or more every day.

We'll also have to improve our vision. Think again of Elizabeth Barrett Browning: "Earth's crammed with heaven, / And every common bush afire with God." We too often think that heaven touches earth only rarely, perhaps once or twice in a person's lifetime. Miss Browning knew better; she knew that earth is *crammed* with heaven. And she knew it because she had come to realize that every common bush is "afire with God"—which, I suppose, is to declare that "common bush" is an oxymoron; there is no such thing as a *common* bush. Every bush is uncommon.

I like Mike Mason's report: "Sometimes in the woods I'll see a wildflower, perhaps one that has just blossomed that morning, and I'll think: *No one has ever laid eyes on this flower before*" (italics in the original).[6] This is the true Eden mood. On any given morning, you and I step out into a new world, fresh from the hands of the Creator. We speak with proper awe of those settlers who broke virgin soil to plant seed where no human hand had ever planted it before. But the world into which we step each day—or even the flowers that a city dweller nurtures on an apartment rooftop or in a window box—is new today. Catch that bird song! It is only once, and it is for you, today. The bird will sing it again for some other attentive soul, and another bird will sing tomorrow, but today's aria is for you, if you will receive it. This morning is Eden! Don't miss it.

This was the mood of that anonymous Hebrew poet who cried, "Bless the LORD, O my soul," and then began telling us why: He (or she) noticed that "springs gush forth in the valleys," and from God's "lofty abode you water the mountains." "The trees of the LORD are watered abundantly.... In them the birds build their nests" (Psalm 104:1, 10, 13, 16-17). Wherever the psalmist looked, there God was at work. I don't know where the psalmist lived the rest of that day, but for a while, he was living in Eden.

By now you've come to realize, if you've stayed with me all the way, that this is not a book of science; it is intended only to make nature our dear friend, and in the process to know God better. The goal is to see the wonders of nature, yes, but not to see them as ends in themselves, impressive as they are, but to enjoy what they tell us about God and life and ourselves. And then, to reenter Eden every morning.

It isn't easy, of course. The poet-preacher with whom we entered this book, Maltbie Babcock, prayed, "O let me ne'er forget / that though the wrong seems oft so strong, / God is the ruler yet." Some days, we have to speak such words with particular emphasis.

The poet Joseph Auslander tells the story of the last lecture George Santayana gave at Harvard. Santayana was not only one of the most challenging philosophers of his time, he was also a brilliant lecturer, so that his classes had become legendary. On a day in April, he was giving his last lecture, and it was a true tour de force. Suddenly, in the middle of a sentence—in truth, in the very middle of a line—Santayana caught sight of a forsythia pushing its way through a patch of muddy snow just outside the classroom window. He stopped; picked up his hat, his gloves, and his walking stick; and started out of the lecture room. At the door, he turned back to the class. "Gentlemen," he said, "I shall not be able to finish that sentence. I have just discovered that I have an appointment with April."[7]

When you see your forsythia—or perhaps your violet or dandelion—I hope you'll spend a moment in Eden.

NOTES

1. Eleanor Farjeon, *Something I Remember* (London: Puffin Books, 1989), 5-6.

2. Gerard Manley Hopkins, *God's Grandeur and Other Poems* (New York: Dover Publications, 1995), 15.

3. *The New Interpreter's Study Bible* (Nashville: Abingdon Press, 2003), 9.

4. Ursula Goodenough, *The Sacred Depths of Nature* (Oxford: Oxford University Press, 1998), 168.

5. Sinclair Lewis, *Babbitt* (New York: Harcourt, Brace and Company, 1922), 148.

6. Mike Mason, *Practicing the Presence of People* (Colorado Springs: Waterbrook Press, 1999), 55.

7. Cleveland Amory, *Holiday*; quoted in *The Christian Leader's Golden Treasury* (New York: Grosset & Dunlap, 1955), 356.

DISCUSSION GUIDE FOR *ALL CREATION SINGS: THE VOICE OF GOD IN NATURE*

by J. Ellsworth Kalas

John D. Schroeder

CHAPTER 1
ALL NATURE SINGS

Snapshot Summary
This chapter explores God's hand in nature and shows us how to hear nature's voice, as well as God's voice in nature.

Reflection/Discussion Questions
1. Share your interest in this book and what you hope to gain from your experience of reading and discussing this book.
2. Reflect on/discuss the meaning of the phrase "all nature sings."
3. Share a time when you heard nature's voice. What made it so memorable?
4. Why is it more difficult to hear nature's voice today? Name a few of the obstacles.
5. How did biblical writers view nature, and how was their view of nature reflected in their writing?
6. Name some ways or examples in which believers have seen God's hand in nature.
7. What did the Apostle Paul say about the revelation of God in nature?

8. Reflect on/discuss how our power of choice distinguishes us from the rest of creation.

9. Name some ways in which nature declares the glory of God.

10. What additional thoughts or ideas from this chapter would you like to explore?

Prayer: *Dear God, thank you for the wonders of nature and for being able to enjoy all the sights and sounds of your creation. Help us appreciate nature more, be more protective of it, and learn the lessons it has to teach us. Amen.*

CHAPTER 2
THE STORY OF THE THREE TREES

Snapshot Summary
This chapter looks at the tree of the knowledge of good and evil, the tree of life, and the tree of Calvary, and why each is important.

Reflection/Discussion Questions
1. Share your thoughts about a tree that was or is special to you.

2. What does the author tell us about the "holy history" of trees?

3. What is known about the tree of the knowledge of good and evil in the Garden of Eden?

4. According to the author, what issue does the tree of knowledge represent to us today, and why?

5. Reflect on/discuss Dietrich Bonhoeffer's insight that "the only visible sign of God in the world is the cross."

6. Describe the pros and cons Adam and Eve faced regarding eating fruit from the tree of the knowledge of good and evil.

7. Reflect on/discuss the tree of life, which is described in the book of Revelation.

8. What is the "third tree" the author discusses, and why is it important?

9. Reread the last sentence in this chapter, and answer its question.

10. What additional thoughts or ideas from this chapter would you like to explore?

Prayer: *Dear God, thank you for using trees to touch our lives. May we remember the holy history of trees and the role they have played in your creation. Help us appreciate this gift of your creation. Amen.*

CHAPTER 3
THE NOT-SO-DUMB OX

Snapshot Summary

This chapter uses the ox to teach us about reasoning and the expectations God has for us.

Reflection/Discussion Questions

1. What does the author say regarding slang and figures of speech?

2. Why is the ox a remarkable creature and not so dumb?

3. How has the phrase "dumb ox" been used in the past, and what does it mean today?

4. The author points out that unlike the ox, we humans have the ability to reason. Give some examples of how we ignore reason.

5. If the ox could speak, what do you believe it might say about us humans?

6. Explain why God expects us to *understand* and to use our mental abilities.

7. Discuss the "family reasoning" that God seeks and expects from us.

8. Reflect on/discuss the following statement: "All of us

know something about the reason of relationship from common experiences."

9. Why do we need "our reasoning to be more reasonable," as the author suggests? How might this happen?

10. What additional thoughts or ideas from this chapter would you like to explore?

Prayer: *Dear God, thank you for the ability to reason, to know right from wrong, and to be so full of potential and creativity. Forgive us when we ignore reason, make unwise decisions, and hurt others in the process. Help us use the wisdom you have provided all of us. Amen.*

CHAPTER 4
FASHION SHOW IN A FIELD

Snapshot Summary
This chapter explores the beauty in nature, as evidenced in the flowers of the field, and the importance of having inner beauty.

Reflection/Discussion Questions
1. Share your thoughts on why people are interested in or worry about clothing.

2. Describe the clothing worn by people in the time of Jesus. How was this clothing very practical and functional?

3. Reflect on/discuss the beauty and life of the common flower, as observed by Jesus.

4. How are we different from, yet also the same as, the lilies of the field?

5. Reflect on/discuss why beauty treatments—"those things we put on from the outside," as the author describes them—are often self-centered and self-defeating.

6. Explain what is meant by the author's remark that "the lily is unself-conscious."

7. Name some things that endanger or destroy beauty in our world today.
8. Why can't the best of beauty be purchased?
9. Name some lessons we can learn from the flowers in the field.
10. What additional thoughts or ideas from this chapter would you like to explore?

Prayer: *Dear God, thank you for the beauty of flowers and for the lessons about true beauty in this chapter. Help us nurture beauty in ourselves and in others, while we learn what the beauty of nature has to teach us. Amen.*

CHAPTER 5
A GOOD WORD FOR THE SPIDER

Snapshot Summary
This chapter uses the spider to show us the expectations God has for us and what we should do with our talents.

Reflection/Discussion Questions
1. Prior to reading this chapter, what were your thoughts or feelings about spiders?
2. Share some interesting facts about the spider as found in this chapter.
3. What wisdom and skills has God given the spider?
4. What do spiders and humans have in common?
5. In what ways does God want us to be different from spiders?
6. Discuss the author's observations about cattle grazing.
7. God expects us to make use of what we are given. Name some of the things God has given us.
8. Name some reasons why we do not use what God has given us.
9. The author says that, unlike spiders, "We humans bear

the burden of questions and struggles of the soul." Reflect on/discuss this aspect of life and its implications.
10. What additional thoughts or ideas from this chapter would you like to explore?

Prayer: *Dear God, thank you for the unique wisdom and skills you have given each of us. Help us put this potential to good use. May we learn from the spider and from all creatures the role we all play in your world. Amen.*

CHAPTER 6
WHEN THE TREES HELD AN ELECTION

Snapshot Summary
This chapter examines the parable of an election by trees and provides insights into government, politicians, and voting.

Reflection/Discussion Questions
1. What stories about nature and animals did you enjoy as a child?
2. Share your thoughts about the story of the day the trees held an election (Judges 9:8-15).
3. What is known about Jotham, the storyteller? What are your thoughts about him?
4. What message was Jotham perhaps trying to get across?
5. The author tells us that this parable about the day the trees held an election frightens him. Do you share his feelings? Explain.
6. Can being a politician be a calling under God? Share your thoughts.
7. How do you think God feels about politics and political leaders today?
8. What qualities make a good leader?
9. Why do you vote in elections? If you don't vote, what could be the consequences?

10. What additional thoughts or ideas from this chapter would you like to explore?

Prayer: *Dear God, thank you for the opportunity to elect those who govern us. Help us take the right to vote seriously and encourage others to do the same. May we be responsible citizens and leaders. Amen.*

CHAPTER 7
AS FAIR AS THE RAIN

Snapshot Summary

This chapter reminds us of the impartiality of nature and uses the words of Jesus to encourage us to treat others generously and impartially.

Reflection/Discussion Questions

1. Share your own evidence for or insights into the remarkable generosity of nature.
2. Regarding generosity in nature, what message did Jesus give to his listeners, and why?
3. Why is it so difficult to pray for those who persecute us?
4. Reflect on/discuss the meaning and implications of Matthew 5:45, where Jesus notes the impartiality of nature.
5. Why are God and nature impartial? Why are we not as impartial?
6. Why did the preaching of Jesus make many people uncomfortable?
7. Have people changed at all since the time of Jesus in how they view and act toward enemies? Explain your answer.
8. Reflect on/discuss the meaning of *agape* love, and give an example of it.
9. What did you learn about love and God's love from reading this chapter?
10. What additional thoughts or ideas from this chapter would you like to explore?

Prayer: *Dear God, thank you for showing us what it means to be impartial, and for the power of agape love. Help us learn from the example of nature to be generous and impartial. Amen.*

CHAPTER 8
LIVING IN HIGH PLACES

Snapshot Summary
This chapter teaches us how to use our faith in God to guide our steps following the examples of deer, Habakkuk, and King David.

Reflection/Discussion Questions
1. Share what comes to mind when you hear the word *deer*.
2. List and discuss references to deer found in the psalms.
3. Why did David feel God had blessed him with feet like those of a deer?
4. Share what we know of Habakkuk and the world in which he lived.
5. Why did Habakkuk call on God for help? What was God's answer?
6. What impresses you about Habakkuk's declaration of faith?
7. What was Habukkuk's secret, as described in Habakkuk 3:19?
8. Where does surefootedness of the soul come from? How do you get "feet like a deer"?
9. Explain what the author means by the statement that being a Christian means living in high places.
10. What additional thoughts or ideas from this chapter would you like to explore?

Prayer: *Dear God, thank you for reminding us of the wisdom of David and Habakkuk as we face difficult times in life. Help us re-*

member we can have feet like deer and live in high places when we trust in you. Amen.

CHAPTER 9
AN ANT IN THE PULPIT

Snapshot Summary
This chapter shows how the tiny ant provides us with big lessons about work, jobs, and what God wants us to do with our lives.

Reflection/Discussion Questions
1. According to the author, what did Benjamin Franklin say about the ant, and why might Franklin's words be inspired by Proverbs 6:6-9?
2. Give some words or phrases that describe the ant.
3. Why does the author refer to the ant as a miracle?
4. The author tells us, "Carl Sandburg imagined God as a worker." Do you view God the same way? Explain your answer.
5. Reflect on/discuss the sacredness of work. Do we usually treat work as sacred? Why or why not?
6. List and discuss some of the many questions the author raises about work and workers.
7. Share how you feel about your job or a job that you held in the past.
8. Describe the benefits of work and a job well done.
9. What are the most important lessons we can we learn from ants?
10. What additional thoughts or ideas from this chapter would you like to explore?

Prayer: *Dear God, thank you for giving us work to do while we are living in your world. Help us remember that work is sacred, and that doing your work furthers your kingdom. Amen.*

CHAPTER 10
A BUSH THAT BURNS AND BURNS

Snapshot Summary
This chapter uses the story of Moses and the burning bush to focus on those life-changing moments we all experience.

Reflection/Discussion Questions
1. Share a memorable or life-changing event from your life. Do you connect memorable moments as signs from God?
2. Reflect on/discuss what you believe life is like for a shepherd. What are some of the advantages and disadvantages of the profession?
3. How did Moses become a shepherd? What had he done?
4. According to the author, why are bushes largely ignored, particularly as compared with trees?
5. How did Moses encounter the burning bush? How did he react?
6. What message did God deliver to Moses through the burning bush? What was Moses' reply?
7. How did Elizabeth Barrett Browning view the story of Moses and the burning bush?
8. The author asks the question, "Does every human being sometime, somewhere, see a bush that burns?" How would you answer that question?
9. What forms can a burning bush take for us, and how can such an experience be life-changing?
10. What additional thoughts or ideas from this chapter would you like to explore?

Prayer: *Dear God, thank you for the many ways in which you speak to us and help us do your will. Help us keep our eyes and ears open for your messages and direction. Just as you spoke to Moses, you speak to each of us today. Amen.*

CHAPTER 11
THE UNIVERSE WITHIN

Snapshot Summary
This chapter looks at the wonders of nature and shows how each of us is a wonderful creation of God.

Reflection/Discussion Questions
1. Share where you would like to go to view the wonders of God in nature.
2. Name a wonder of God that has always impressed you. What makes this wonder impressive?
3. What realization does the psalmist come to while looking at the stars (Psalm 8:3-4)?
4. Why do we often overlook how remarkable, as God's creations, humans really are?
5. List some of the wonders mentioned by the psalmist.
6. Which thoughts from the author about how remarkable people are impressed you the most?
7. Name some of the wonders of the human body.
8. In what ways has God "invested the divine image in us"?
9. What is the best way to thank God for creating us as remarkable creatures?
10. What additional thoughts or ideas from this chapter would you like to explore?

Prayer: *Dear God, thank you for the wonder and the miracle that is each of us. Help us value our uniqueness and our potential. May we strive to live remarkable lives. Amen.*

CHAPTER 12
EDEN EVERY MORNING

Snapshot Summary
This chapter looks at the wonder of Eden and how it exists for us today in nature and within our souls.

Reflection/Discussion Questions

1. Share the title of a poem or a story that you loved as a child and describe why you loved this particular work.
2. Why do you think a poem like "Morning Has Broken" is beloved by so many?
3. Reflect on/discuss why thoughts of Eden speak to us so deeply.
4. Name some things we can learn from nature and tell how this learning process takes place. What must we do to learn?
5. How can we be good stewards of nature? Name some simple ways we can be nature's friend.
6. Reflect on/discuss the price we are paying for "progress" today.
7. Explain what is meant by the statement that "we all have that touch of Eden in our souls."
8. List some ways in which we can claim Eden every morning.
9. Why do adults often lose their appetite for Eden?
10. What additional thoughts or ideas from this chapter would you like to explore?

Prayer: *Dear God, thank you for the opportunity to live with you in Eden. Help us be good caretakers of nature and learn to see nature as a gift as well as a friend and ally. Amen.*